FULL CIRCLE

THE 360 DEGREE PHLIOSOPHY

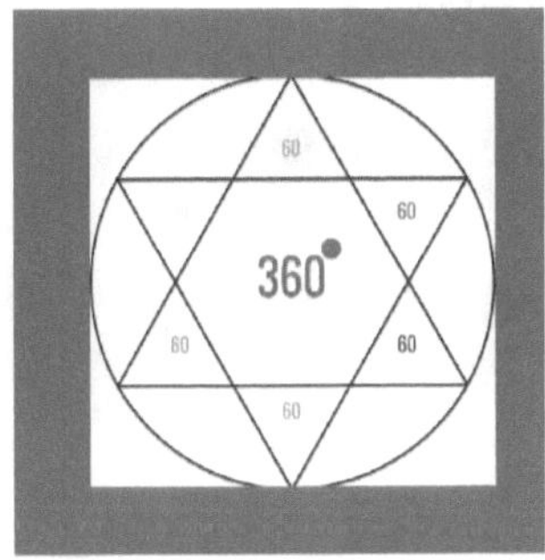

By Terry Byas

Table of Contents

PROLOGUE

This book is about the philosophy of the FULL CIRCLE. The things that are spoken about in this book, is about balance, resurrection, corrections of the misguided mind state of the society that we live in. While reading, it may seem like the person who wrote this book is all over the place. However, they do have some very profound things to say. There will be things that will offend the reader, especially if it has something to do with their life. So, let's go on the journey of the FULL CIRCLE and enter the mind of the author.

CHAPTER 1
60 Degrees

"Blow you nose from the busy body of other people's affairs, which have nothing to do in your realm of existence."

The Beginning/These Jobs aren't Loyal

The beginning of the life cycles we start with, is using the ability to find our way to the full circle of our existence. The first thing we must recognize, is the ability to adapt ourselves to the environment that we were born in. In such, the ability to use the modern-day barter system. That we as humans, created the jobs with the businesses that were started. To produce goods and services in the shift of the cycles that are moved around the world.

The thought of fulfillment enters the human mind to make sense of this cycle of life. With that, once you realize the job you are doing, is not the freedom you want. Due to every so-called career you have, everything you build up can be destroyed with the stroke of a pen or the sound of the words, "we decided to terminate your employment with the company." You will find yourself falling out of balance, due to the murder of your self-esteem in some else's hands. Also, the suicide of your own self-worth in yours. I came to the realization to the full circle of my existence, through meditation in a quiet place of the recesses in my mind and through the revelations of the energies of the universe. This divine intervention was the key that opened the door to my mind to understanding, what were the degrees of existence in which we call life.

Mirror/Repeating

When you look in the mirror of your degree of existence, you will find yourself in the reflection of your own decisions and the actions that follow. In which, you must think logically when you make these decisions and commit these actions, which will affect those that are around you. That is when you can go to the next degree of your existence. Life is a never-ending circle of repeats. It goes around in the infinite cycle with no end in sight and with a repeated beginning, end and back to the beginning, which is a resurrection. When you stop and look at the surroundings of where you stand, you should wonder where it all come from. It could be where you live, who your parents are and how the issues of your life ever manifested in the tangible reality. We have heard the saying, "there's nothing new under the sun." This is a true statement, when you see and do things that were done, before you were born. You will feel like you are stuck in a constant Déjà vu of events that you'll think, "wait a minute I done this before, or I've seen this before." When that happens, you will come to that realization of everything is repeated in the constant circular loop.

Everything is a repeat of different degrees of ideologies, technology, and actions. These things are needed, to be born out of a necessity to manifest "new to you" ideologies. To live in an everyday existence of the universal need to bring new ideas, thoughts and actions that make us who we are and how we live in this world while we are here. If no one listens to the exchange of the continuous ideas and thoughts for this cycle of existence. Then the circle of balance that is within each of us, will be tossed off the axis of our stability and drift into the void of the space that it once was in before.

Wisdom Transference

When I was at work the other day, I was employed at a health insurance company, not going to name which one but it rhymes with B. Ross and Stu Fields I digress. I was speaking to a member. We were conversing about how the health insurance was back in his day such as how it paid, what was needed before an authorization for a surgery among other things. While we were talking, he said something that sparked the exchange of the ideas from the elder to the younger.

This is the cycle of the past generation giving their ideas to the new generation. One day you will find yourself in the same position as the older passing your wisdom to the younger. This is the continuous circle of passing wisdom, knowledge and understanding. It is never-ending and there is always something new to the person hearing it. Hearing these things, will have you understanding what is coming in your life when the songs of wisdom is whispering in your ear. Only a fool will not heed to the wisdom of the correct direction of the circle of your existence. When you do not take the lessons that you hear and apply them to your life, then the intellect that you have is for naught. They're a lot of smart people in dire straits, due to the wisdom of the past where not used for the future. They had to suffer the consequences of deafness that they had, for the wisdom not to be heard.

Watch Yourself

Clean out your ears from the wax of stubbornness. Take out the dirt of instability and confusion. Unplug from the clogged air of the unrelenting sense of arrogance of not wanting to hear the wisdom from the infinite circles that were before you. So, you can pass it to the ones that will come after you. Wash the dirt from your eyes to use the sense of sight, so that you can see what is in front of you. Put on the glasses to correct your vision of the issues in your life. Also, wear sunglasses when someone else's brightness of their inadequacies tries to shine into your night.

Blow you nose from the busy body of other people's affairs, which have nothing to do in your realm of existence. When you worry about what is going on around and not what's going on within you, then your mirror the so-called perfection of a life that is not yours. Keep your square perpendicular to the ground that you walk on. So, you know what is the spark that is in you, to wash off the make-up in the mirror and see your true reflection for who you really are and the reality of things. That is the onion of your essence to peel back the layers of the plague, so you can find a cure of the disease that you have been living with. When you pluck out the weeds of your garden of serenity, happiness, and the all-over copacetic nature of your life, you shall know true peace within yourself. Let it be known, you say to your mirror that is the reflection that you were born with, "the only thing that can affect me is what I allow." In life that would save you a whole lot of stress that you don't need. When you look at this from the prospective of what other people do that would affect them, doesn't affect you and it is irrelevant to your existence.

We all have choices

Every choice count whether you think is the correct one or not. They're many things that we put to a choice daily such as; what shirt to wear, what to eat, how to wear our hair. Do you want to get married or divorced? Do you want to start a dating relationship, or do you want to end one? These are the choices that may seem minute for the one who is not making the choices but normal for the person who must make these kinds of choices daily.

Speaking of the normalcy of the decisions that must be made and the fact some of the choices may not seem normal from the outside. It reminds me what Morticia Addams said in an episode of the TV show the Addams Family, "Normal is an illusion, what is normal for the spider is chaos to the fly." That quote describes an everyday existence of lifestyles, actions, types of languages that are spoken, health, types of food we eat and how the relationships that are outside of you have with their partners.

Logic

I was talking to a fellow student in my class and we were talking about polygyny and polyandry relationships. She was saying how she was kind of offended at the notion of one man with multiple women (polygyny) instead of one woman with multiple men (polyandry). So, I asked her what is wrong with one man and multiple women she said, "I think that it is a double standard in society that when a woman is with multiple men then it is wrong for her to do that but, if one man is with multiple women he is praised for being a so-called real man." I said to her, "well it goes like this, think about a garden or a farm and you want to plant some flowers to beautify your garden and the farmer want to plant corn for the upcoming harvest season. You till your ground and the farmer till theirs. You plant your seed in one spot and the farmer plant the seeds in one spot of the field when that plant fully grows and the farmers corn fully grows, the farmer harvest the one stock of corn and try to plant another flower or seed in the same spot. Well the garden will not be beautified; the farmer will starve. However, if the gardener and the farmer plant multiple seeds in different parts of the fields, then the garden will be full, the harvest would be plentiful. That is why it is logical for one man to have multiple women and not one woman with multiple men."

Telling that story is a constant reminder of what was said in the earlier paragraphs, that what may seem like a double standard and strange in the so-called societal norm. However, it could be the best decision that person would make in their lives and only the person who makes that choice is the one who will have to live with it. "Do it thou wilt" that is what Allister Crowley said, it means to do what you do for your life to be complete and have no regards of what others may think. That is what I got out of it. We have cared what other people thought since the beginning of time, from when the first humans came out of the continent that we call Africa. Every day we look for other ways to show others, that we care about their opinions.

Stop Caring

We need to stop that; there was a video about how other people opinions and what they think are irrelevant. There was this quote by Martha Graham, she said, "what other people in the world think of you is really none of your business." That one quote says a lot, about how we take things other people say about our life decisions to heart. Meanwhile, we should take what they say with a grain of salt. If people like the founders of businesses such as the founder of Primerica Art Williams, thought of what other people thought about buying term and invest the difference. Meanwhile, other insurance companies where just taking their clients' money and selling insurance policies such as whole life, universal life and other various products and not telling the truth. About the fact, they do not get the cash value of the policy just the benefit amount. Also, if they borrow from the cash value they must pay back, if the policy holder that borrowed on the cash value died then it comes out of the benefit amount. Including what interest that accumulated on the borrowed amount, then Primerica would have never existed.

Also, other founders such as Colonel Sanders who founded Kentucky Fried Chicken at the age of 62, people laughed at him saying that he was too old to start a business and people are not going to spend money buying fried chicken. Now, KFC has restaurants all over the U.S and several foreign countries. Bill Gates is another name that comes to mind when we founded Microsoft, Steve Jobs who founded Apple and Robert L. Johnson and Shelia Johnson who founded the Afro-American entertainment channel B.E.T. (Black Entertainment Television).

People said to them that it would never work, nobody would want to watch it, it is still around present day. Also, the founder of the wresting entertainment company WWF (World Wrestling Federation) now WWE (World Wrestling Entertainment) Vincent McMahon Sr and went over to his son Vincent McMahon Jr. People said it would never work when he founded the company but now it still exists and other wrestling companies that tried to compete are no longer around. I am talking about these people to say that, if they cared what other people thought and they took their "grain-of-salt" truths to their inner beings. Then these companies, the people who work or have worked for these companies, would never had the opportunities with these companies. Also, these companies would not have existed.

The reason that most people of society have their opinions about what is outside of them, is the same reason why some people like eating meat and some people do not. It is different from the norm of the rose-colored glasses of their image, of what they have been a part of. Just like when I see debates of Atheist (those who do not have the belief of a deity without enough evidence of one) and Theist (those who believe in a deity in faith). I listen to both sides for their justification of their beliefs or lack of evidence of that said belief. In my opinion, there isn't a winner or loser of these debates, but a conceding of the debate when one does not make their point. Such as when Theist Ken Ham and Bill Nye had this debate about the exist of said deity. Bill Nye was on the position of there's not enough evidence of a deity. That everything thing can be explained with rational thought and provable evidence and not say, "God did it." Ken Ham was on the position of God is the foundation of the universe, the earth was created only 6000 years ago from the story of Adam and Eve. Also, everything from the Bible is true and evolution is a myth.

I listened to their points; it was a split from the point of view of the ones listening to the debate. There were no concessions of the debate, this debate between deity believers and non-believers is still going on to this day. Telling that story, means that the opinions of others based on such things, are changeable and isn't etched in stone, nor is it solidified in the thoughts of those who have them. Choices must be made, actions must be taken, and opinions will be given, even when no one asked for them. The actions of others should not affect you when it has nothing to do with you. If, it is not causing you harm and they are living their life the best way they see fit. Allow them to live their life and whatever choices they make, is the one that they will have to play out. Also, right, or wrong is a matter of opinion.

Yesterday's Trash

Growing up, I had other people tell me about their opinion of me and the choices I made and the actions that I did. For instance, girls I were with, friends I made and activities I were in. Somewhere good and I took those with the same mindset as I took the negative ones, with a grain of salt. There was this one woman I was with; she was to others which you would call stuck up and anti-social to those who she felt that was not even worth her breath. This is where opinions of others are about the incorrect belief of a person. She was not stuck up she was observant. She looked at the behaviors of others to tell who friend or foe were. I first met her when I was in Job Corp in Utah and she was there about 2 months before I came there.

We dated until she graduated, she was a nice person once I broke through that shell she had. People saw us, they would tell her that I was not good enough and others would tell me that she wasn't the person that she "pretended" to be, but I knew better. Telling that story is exactly the reason that a person's choices, actions, and opinions are left to the ones, who is in the mist of those who are making them. This is just one of the parts of the infinite circle of existence. That we must have continuous reasons to make our decisions and actions that follow them, the very thing that can lead us to the paths that can be taken.

CHAPTER 2

120 DEGREES

"How you feel about something is a choice not a crutch. You're not the victim, you're the perpetrator of your own imagination."

Decisions

You are coming to the fork of the road of your life. You must decide which path do you want to take, which choice will you make, which action will you commit for the days of your life. Also, which opinion will you take with the filters of the dirt, from the gold nuggets of reason in the deep conscious of your mind. Will you let it affect you, to the point you are knocked off your foundation of the house of self-esteem that you have built. Or, will you allow the construction crumble, under the pressure of the strong hands of others that don't want you to succeed. Only you can make the choices, only you can commit the actions that are for your life. Only you can make the thought, of how you want your life to manifest into the tangible existence of your success or failure. There are many things we go through that can have a dramatization of our lives through the eyes of others, the decisions and actions that we commit to like a faithful marriage are the reasons we should not allow our lives, our stories and the facts of our existing nature of living to be dictated by others who are not in the space of our realm.

Hero's and Villain's. Angels and Devils.

Victims and the perpetrators are in the same realm of existence. When one becomes the perpetrator of their thought process, they make victims of themselves. To the point, they look for someone to take on their essence, to surround them in the darkness that is the black hole of their existence. When I was on my business page on Facebook, I felt like posting one of my thoughts and in this post I was sparked by a dream of inspiration of something I went through, the quote said "how you feel about something is a choice not a crutch, you're not the victim, you're the perpetrator of your own imagination". For years I felt like I was victimized by this person, due to our relationship ended in a way that broke me down to the point of I didn't want to be in another relationship again. I felt that it would always end the same way and I would have to start all over with a new woman. At the time I was going through this, I had a low opinion of women in general. It seemed like every time I looked around; some woman is always the perpetrator of a man's outlook on the next relationship, he has with the next woman. Also, they turned good men into the scum of the earth.

I felt this way for years. I analyzed and scrutinized every woman I came across. I felt that if anything happened to them, such as if their men were mad at them, I would first blame the woman. If a man hit them, the first question I would ask is, "what did that woman do for that man to act like that towards her, she had to do something?" Over the years as I am reminiscing as I am writing this book, I'm glad I no longer have those thoughts or the low opinions about women due to what I went through with my ex-wife. She is an individual not the entire female species.

When I posted that quote it sent chills in my mind due to, I have never thought of anything like that when I was going through that situation at that time. However, now as I'm no longer in the space of the bitterness of my galaxy, I have a very clear understanding that we are only victims if we allow the perpetrators of the dark alley of our minds to have power over us. Never give your light to someone who is dim in the spirit and dark in the heart.

Time is still ticking

"Time is of the essence," how many times have we heard that during our lives, did anyone ever stop and think what that saying really meant below the surface of the shallow thought. We say things like that, but never stop to think how it would apply to our lives. Which the saying, should apply to the lives of everyone on this Earth due to, one day the measure of time stops at the finish line of our existence. The modern clock is a physically manifestation of the measure of time, just like the sun dial of the olden days and the movement of the sun and moon dictates when one day passes and a new day rises.

As we measure the time we have on this Earth, there is no slowing of the clock, no going back and no fast forward, it moves at a pace that is dictated by the shift of the environments that we are in. Texas, the state I live in, we are in the central time zone. The east coast it is 1 hour ahead of us, mountain time is an hour behind us, and the coastal west of the U.S. is 2 hours behind us. In many countries that are east of the Atlantic are at the most 9 hours ahead of us, the ones that are west of the Atlantic are at most 9 hours behind us. This measurement of time, is according to the state or country you are in. It is also dictated, by the jobs or activities that we do daily. We must look at this for what is really is, it is something not to be wasted on the remembrance of bad times, the storms, the pains, and sorrows of situations that have long since passed.

I remember growing up going to church and reading religious texts. I would always sit there and think about, when will this service be over. The church I went to, had the 7:00 and the 11:00am services. I always went to the 7:00 when I could, because I didn't want to sit there for the whole day. One day, I was looking at the clock on the side wall, expecting the ending of this service. I could have sworn, I seen the hands of the clock go 5 minutes back, to lengthen the time that I would have to be there. Then I remember that that is impossible for time to go backwards, due to if that was the case, we would get younger instead of getting older. The Curious Case of Benjamin Button was a movie that I saw at least 5 times. This movie wasn't like any other movie I ever seen. This movie was original, no one ever had the idea before that time to make a movie from the short story by F. Scott Fitzgerald. From his Tales of the Jazz collection, which was genius. I digress, it was a story about a boy being born with a rare disease that had him age in reverse from old to young. Watching that movie, got me analyzing it while I was watching. The conclusion I came to was this; the way we were born is exactly the way we die, with the mind and the helplessness as a newborn.

Unfortunately, things are that way, measurable time is not something we can halt in its tracks. We get older by the second, minute, hour, day, months, and years. "Life is too short," I know it seems like a cliché that we've all heard before, but that saying is true. Life is too short for anything that we may go through. We allow it to affect us, that we hold on to it for so long, it seems we would not survive it without the parasite of its existence. Parasites cannot survive without a host if the host is alive the parasite will stay attached. We as humans, can't allow the parasites of jealousy, envy, hatred, and the overall bitterness of failed relationships to affect us. We waste all our time and effort thinking about it.

There was a young lady that I used to go out to lunch with, when we used to work at the same employer. We used to have very interesting conversations about life and past relationships. I could tell every time, when she talks about her past relationships, it was still fresh on her mind about what happened in those relationships. What she was telling me that, whenever that every guy that she wanted to date always wanted to be friends, never called her back, or kept her at arms distance. She felt a way about those relationships, these weren't recent events, these were events that happened at least 5 years from that time. I could see the pain and anguish in her eyes. She had spent all her time thinking about those situations so much, that when it came to relationships, she had pretty much given up on the notion of have any kind of meaningful relationship with a man. She expected the same thing to happen over and over as a repeating sequence of events of the Groundhog Day dating scene.

Having those lunches with her taught me something, when relationships end or for whatever reason don't start in the way that you would want them to start. Do not waste time dwelling on the finite system of those that are not interested, instead look at the infinite possibilities of potential fruit ready for you to pluck it from the tree of reciprocation. Time is ticking, the sand of your hourglass is running out, the second hand is moving to count the minutes and the minute hands are counting the hours and each hour that comes you will go into the next day from the earlier. Never take for granted, that we have all the time in the world. To think that we can still look at the pass, as a new scene to an event, that we can look at without a life lesson.

While we are looking at what it was instead what can be, we will strain ourselves thinking about pass events that will never happen again. I was speaking to a co-worker and I said that since this was a new year, "what was will never be again." Meaning that whatever happened that had us in a sense of despair, to a point that we were so low that we had to stand up in Hell to look down in Heaven. The smoke has cleared, the time has passed and the things that had you in that state at that time. The clouds have parted, the sun is shining, it's a new dawn, it is a new day and you have made it through. Do you remember the song, "The sun will come out tomorrow"?

As I grew older, I thought of that song in the context of whatever happened in the night that dimed your internal light, for you to see the way out of the dark alley. You need to move towards that light that once shined brightly. When it is so dark, you can't see in front of your hands. When you reach your hands out, you can feel your happiness slipping through your fingers. Grasp the walls of your life, so you wouldn't be sucked into the black hole of the eternal darkness.

There's no going back/Tear down the Walls

The next day is here and the sun has come out, the chance to start a new day. Do not look in the rearview mirror of the earlier because you can't go back and unlike a video game there isn't a reset. One day I was in my office doing a project, I started thinking about past events and how it can the past could affect the present that you are in if you allow it. The reason I say, "if you allow it," is due to the past, the time that goes with it. Can only affect you, if you allow everything that happened, to get you to put up a wall bigger than the one Trump is trying to build.

When you build the walls of defense based on pass experiences, you think you're protecting yourself. You've had experiences that traumatized you, to the point where you think no one can be trusted. You live on the philosophy of D.T.A. (Don't Trust Anybody), justifiably so, but that's only good for a while. Then you would be at the point of no return to block those out of your life. Those who aren't like the people that have hurt you, it would be hurtful for you do that. The reason that this is being said, is that the time you spend on thinking about the pass hurts, time will continue. You will get older, meanwhile you're still hanging on to the bull*hit that had you in that state of dismissing BLESSED BE's out of your life. That could have been the person or people, which would have planted the seed in your soul, to get you back to the time of when you were at your highest point.

Events such as a death in the family, can really put any issue in prospective when it comes to anything that you are holding on to. We live like we're immortal and say to ourselves that issues can be solved later. Whatever unforgiveness we had harbored in our hearts for family members, can be talked about when it is convenient. When a family member, whom you had issues with dies. Your mind races with all the could of, would of and should of's. Then afterwards there is nothing left to do but lift your head and talk with the quite sky.

While you are holding on to the pain the clock is still ticking with no change in sight, before you know a lot of time has passed. No one looks the same, you got older, the old got older, your little nieces and nephews are almost adults and the physicality of your hometown has changed. The climate is different from where you were at. Time is a weight around your neck, that only gets heavier with the issues you put on it. The more weight you put on the time that you have, the more is will be a useless point to lift the heaviness over your head. Most of the weight of your time is not just mental, it can also be physical, emotional, and spiritual, the four points of the compass of your existence.

Shorting your Time is artificial

Such issues that can shorten the time that you have, from a physical standpoint are vices. Such vices as, smoking cigarettes, drinking excessively, doing drugs i.e.; cocaine, crack, and meth, not exercising your body and not eating healthy.   Also, from a mental standpoint such as stress and depression can take a toll on you physically as well. I've seen people who have been through so much stress their health was failing, hair falling out and their bodies were shutting down on them. We must not allow the stresses of life affect us to the point that the time we have is so heavy, that even a ten-pound weight feels like a ton. We must take every chance we get to lighten our load and not add any added weight that we don't need. Such as chains around our necks and shackles on our ankles. So, we don't become enslaved by the need to waste time, by holding on to things that are useless to the prosperity of a fulfilled life.

Earlier I said that time cannot be wasted with harboring the issues that happened years ago. That as long we are holding on to those issues of the past, we can never move forward into our futures. What drives this point on is, if you ever had any conflict with a parent and you didn't get it solved before they left the Earth. Then, you forever will have unresolved issues

between you, all never to be resolved. I have recently lost my mother, now we didn't have any

issues between us, we had our "coming to Jesus" moment. That is not the case with others

who lost their parents or other relatives that they did have issues with. They allowed the

weight of their issues to be heavy with their lives. Also, they allowed these issues to fester like

a rotten apple that's been sitting out on the counter.

Issues can be solved

Thought out the years when I had issues with whom I considered those close to me, I

usually try to solve them. Due to, one day they may not be here before the issue has been

solved. Unfortunately, that was not the case with a close friend of mine whom I introduced to

my best friend, back when we were in high school. Later, they got married and had 4 kids

together. One day my best friend's mother seen me, she informed me that my best friends leg

got amputated due to contracting gangrene from a rusted nail. I haven't seen her for over a

year at that time. Her mother said that they were having a birthday party for her and I knew

this, due to her birthday is almost a month before mine. We were born in the same year. I

went to their house. It was me; her husband, her mother, and a couple of friends were there

celebrating. I couldn't stay long because I had to work the next day, I gave her some birthday

money and kissed her on the cheek. I was walking out, she said that they were barbequing in

the back of the house. I was going to the back yard, her mother came to me and said that her

husband was mad at me for kissing her on the cheek and I shouldn't come back there. I was

puzzled because I was the one who introduced them, so I left, I figured we could solve our issues later. Unfortunately, that time never came, three months later, in July, he had a severe seizure. He hit his head on the headboard on his bed and he died. We didn't even get chance to solve our issues.

That is one story that I tell to hammer the point, that when we think that we have all the time in the world to solve whatever issues that we have with that person or people. We also got to come to the universal realization, that in an instant what takes years that we can resolve the issues that we have. Can remain unresolved in seconds when the last breath is breathed, when the spirit separate from our bodies and when we are gone from this world never to return, at least not how we were. Time ticks, the second-hand moves, the minute hand counts the hour hand changes every sixty minutes. We are not getting any younger, we get older by the hour and each hour gets us closer to our inevitable departure from the world with no return. We must take every second of our lives, look in the space of time that is unfulfilled with the things that cost us every second in our finite existence.

We don't get Younger

As we get older, we should get wiser with the time we have. I remember a verse from a song by a rapper named Too Short. It said, "we can take back all the things we give but we can't take back the days we live." That one verse said exactly how looking back really is. We can never go back not even 5 minutes in the pass to change anything. We should take that realization to understand, that we need to use logic, to not allow the mistakes that we made to overlook what we left behind. Meanwhile, they're mistakes and issues that we did not allow to play out. Till the end of time for the individual lives, that we have on the internal clock of our days, do not let unfortunate circumstances be the only time that we come together.

Case in point; I had to go to Moline, Illinois for my mother's funeral. I haven't been there in almost 10 years. I saw people there I have not seen from the time before I left and some over 10 years ago. I can see the age on their faces, no one looked the same. Could not believe it has been that long, the young got older, the older got older and many generations were at that funeral home. We had our memories and we said our final goodbyes. This also had me thinking, that I never should go this long to see my loved ones, due to what can take years can be finished within seconds. Cherish the moments, you will never get them again.

Our bodies, mentalities, emotions, likes and dislikes for certain lifestyle's, the way we look at society, changes when we move with the forward hands of time. There is a time for everything on the Earth. Time to live, die, laugh, cry, be happy, be sad, depressed, drink, not to drink, letting the world know your thoughts and giving someone the truth pill that is hard to swallow. Flashes of time always happens when you reminisce about the good old days, when we were younger and how things were back in our day. Then when we are done reminiscing about the forward time of days pass, we come back to the living reality that those days. The time that moves forward, the pass is no longer in our reach and forever in the rearview mirror to the drive towards the future.

The time we take to dial a phone number, seconds has passed, the time it takes to listen to your favorite song minutes has passed. The time it takes to hold on to any grudges and not resolve the issue between you and the other person, years has passed. Time doesn't stop, it keeps going, even if you're not here to see it. Day turns to night, night turns into day. We all need to come to the realization, every day that we live time waits for no one in the world. If that was the case, we could go back in time and the mistakes that we have done could be corrected in an instant flash of the desire to change things for the better.

Power to stop time

There was a Twilight Zone episode that was called "A Kind of Stopwatch." The main character had a stopwatch that could stop time in its tracks, also restart with him using the start and stop button on the watch. It was all good until the watch broke and everybody was frozen at the time, he stopped the watch. Even if we had the power to start and time at will to freeze and restart everybody and everything. The one who has that Stopwatch will still get older, due it would be those around them who is frozen, but they would still be the same. That episode taught me that no matter what we do to try pausing the movement of time, there will still be movement of that time. That is the understanding of the FULL CIRCLE, that we must be able to maintain and thrive in life. Never allowing anything to cut the lines of moving with the hands of time.

I remember as a child, I was about 6 years old. My mother sat me down, she said, "Terry there will be a time when I'm no longer here, I'm going to teach you how to take care of yourself." She taught me how to pay bills, cook, clean, do my own laundry, sewing and different decorations that I could do for my house. Now looking back at that memory, I would never forget what she said. That was time well spent, that unfortunately I will never get back.

She was right, she is now gone, and her voice of reason, logic and understanding will linger in

our heart as long we are still breathing. We will pass the lessons that were taught to us, to our

children. They will pass it to their children, in a continuous circle of events of forward moving

time.

Growing Pains/Trivial things

To feel the ages of time moving, is to go through the growing pains of your existence.

We see the bodies of our human understanding change. The time that moves forward is a

double edge sword of being a wonderful thing, to being something that we're not looking

forward too. We waste our time on trivial things such as; the latest gossip on Facebook,

watching "reality" shows, which celebrity is getting a divorce and who's is living the

"alternative" lifestyle. We are not to think about these things, as they're shallow in comparison

to the time we have on this Earth. The whole thought process should be, the time we have is

just as important as quenching your thirst for a prosperous existence.

A prosperous existence is what we all strive for in our lifetime, but we allow the past

experiences that we go through, to hinder our way to a fulfilled life that we can be in control of.

We all have trial and errors that we experience in our lives. However, we need to decide if the

experiences we go through, will they make us stronger than a diamond or weaker than an

airplane hanging on a string. I remember when I heard the Boiling Water analogy, when you

introduce different items to the boiling water the items change. First an egg when it boils it gets firm, vegetables get soft and fall apart. That is to say that depending on how you come out when going through the stresses of life can it make you stronger or will you fall apart when everything hits the fan?

I remember when I was going through my crumbling marriage to my now ex-wife. I have to say that, I have long since then forgave her for her part of the reason that our marriage ended. However, I had to conclude that, we no longer had a relationship or even a friendship. I had to accept that as a point to move on for my own sanity and my spiritual health. At first it made me bitter with life, it had me taking a lot of risk of negative energy transference. That when I came across people that usually I would never even be associated with. I started associating with them and the people I considered my people, I cut them off. So, I had to take a long look in the mirror and say to myself, "I couldn't allow the stresses of the past, turn me into the bitter tasting fruit of my future."

Building Muscle/Back in Time

We workout to get our bodies in shape. Workouts most of the time, consist of lifting weights for strength or to tone the body and running for the cardiovascular system to keep up our stamina. These workouts we do on either daily or on a weekly basis. They make us feel healthier, slimmer, muscular and our blood flows easier. If you think about the workouts and how each time you work out you get stronger, faster and have more alertness in your daily life. Then you will come to the realization that if I used the stresses of my life as I use the workouts to relieve the stresses of my life, then you can say that no matter what I go through in life, it will not make me weak. I will get stronger with everything that happens, because I have the reinforced mentality of not allowing outside issues get inside of my essence.

In the earlier chapter it was discussed about time and the past, every experience we have does coincide with time and the past. There is a movie trilogy called Back to The Future I, II, and III. In these movies the main character traveled back in time when his father and mother were in high school. The events on how his mother and father meet changed with his intervention. When he goes back to his own time, everything changed. His father was a successful self-published author, his older brother had a good job, his sister had every guy after her and his mother looked younger than what she was, and the father's high school bully Biff was washing the father's car and took orders from him.

The question we should ask ourselves is this: if we could go back in time and correct the so-called mistakes of our past, wouldn't you do it? This is the question that should ponder in the dream state of your desire to do things correctly, so you would not make the same mistake twice. If your answer to that question is yes, then only you would know what you would change about your life. Just like the way you live is only for you, that is the in-your-hand power that you will need to move with the rhythm of your existence.

That is all on You

The essence of a prosperous life is to know that the power of the life you live, is based on what you do and how you do it. If you "succeed" in life, then you give credit where credit is due. However, if you "fail," use that same energy to give credit where is due to the so-called failures in your life. We always have someone to blame for the wrongs in our lives but take all the credit for the rights that happen. I remember I was speaking to an old friend of mine about 6 years ago, she was telling me about her relationship and what other things that were going on in her life. While we were conversing, she said that nothing was going right in her life and the "devil" is working.

So, I asked her what is going wrong in her life, she says to me, "I lost my job, the supervisor said that I was late too many times, I'm about to lose my apartment and I don't have anybody to help me with my situation." When I asked her about her relationship with her boyfriend, she informed me they broke up. She didn't mention this when we were speaking earlier. I asked her why they break up, she informed me that it was because she cheated on him. I looked at her with my eyes squinted and wondered; why in the hell did she do that when he was there for her. So, after listening to that I had enough. I told her, "The reason your life isn't going the way you want, it's not because of some 'devil,' that you can't prove the existence of. It's due to, you're the helm of your own ship, but you crashed it into the Titanic of the actions that you did." We do not speak anymore.

Bittersweet Snacks

In the pursuit of a prosperous life, you must take the bitter with the sweet and the truth. Even if it is a chalky pill to swallow. In society, we love to walk around with the rose-colored view of the world to escape the reality that we create. We as humans create the circumstances that we need an escape from. Such as, war, stress, not doing things to the fullest potential, relationships, money, health issues, worrying about the successes or the so-called failures in your life and regrets. With the creation of these thing's from our own hands, we need to realize that we all have a cause and effect choice that is in our control. The control we have over everything we do, is just as powerful as the actions that we manifest from these choices. Case in point; do we really need to kill a bunch of people in a war, where there's no freedom to be had. Not unlike the much-needed slave revolts for the oppressed, but the wars that is for asinine things such as land and resources that no one can ever own.

Another point; do you really need to disturb a relationship by bringing an unwilling or willing participant into the drama, with a one-sided partner? Do we need to cause harm to a person that has never done anything to you, such as rapist, those who harm children, murderers and people who abuse their significant others? We all have a choice to do these things and no one can make those choices, except the person who is choosing to commit the harms of a fellow human being.

Illogical Truth

When I was about 28, when I first came to Texas, there was this couple that I used to work with, they were in the church deeply. One time they invited me to one of their services, I forget the churches name. Afterwards they were introducing me to the members, it was all good until they found out that I was a single man hanging with a married couple. One of the super saver men informed the couple and I that we shouldn't be friends because I was single, and it was temptation. I thought that was an illogical statement.

It has been my experience, that if a married person is going to cheat on their significant other, it will be with another married person or someone who is not expecting that the person they're sleeping with is married. I was about to let him have it, but I kept my composure and let him know that I would never even start a relationship with someone who's married. If anything, I would be the one that would remind that woman that she's married. Also, even though I don't believe in any religions, I do believe that once you're married, there isn't a need to go to an outsider for gratification.

I tell that story to hammer my point, that to have a life that is pleasurable, you must make the choices and commit the actions that you are in control of. That story is an example, that everyone can control every decision that they make. You don't have to bring or keep dangerous thoughts and drama into your life, or into your sanctuary of your mental processes.

When you investigate the thought process of how we as humans make our decisions, we sometimes take on other people negativities and project them on to ourselves. We need to look at the examination of life in the breakdown, of the finest points that are overlooked in the pursuit of living a prosperous life. So, we can block the futile attempt of the overly negative society to project their inadequacies on to you. It can be lonely living a prosperous life. The circle of those who were close to you, will seem like a dot. Especially, when you start telling them that, because their life isn't working for them, that doesn't mean it's not working for me. No one is the same.

Question's

I remember as a child, I was in church for Easter Sunday, I had on my "Easter Suit." The minister at that time was giving a sermon on the death and resurrection of Jesus. The minister said that on Friday he suffered, was killed for all our transgressions as the ultimate sacrifice and on Sunday he was resurrected. As a child, I wondered a few things; 1: why would anybody want to suffer for other people's mistakes, when the very people who made the mistake isn't paying for them? 2: While according to the story, he had to carry his own cross, got whipped while he was doing it. Then get hung up the very cross he had to carry, then die for everyone's wrongs. Didn't he have any thoughts of, "why do I have to do this, when the very 'father' I'm from created everything in the universe. Couldn't my 'father' just forgive everybody that 'he' created." That is what we do daily, we sacrifice ourselves for other people's mistakes and that stops us from living the happy, prosperous, fulfilled life that all of us deserve. Especially in customer service, but that will be another discussion.

Preserve of Self

Self-preservation is the key of living your best life and not worrying about if you're doing enough for someone else. That would be like paying rent or a mortgage for a house that you don't live in. Meanwhile, you're getting your house foreclosed or you're being evicted from your apartment because you aren't paying the bills in your dwelling. I remember when I was younger and going to church. I've always heard that you must look out for your so-called brother and sister in the so-called Christ. However, this is where the contradiction in self-preservation to live the prosperous life comes in. While you're looking to save another person, who's going to be there to save you? The very Bible that most people in church should be reading, should look at saving themselves. Case in point; Ezekiel 18:20 hammers the point of self-preservation when it comes to the so-called sins of another. It says, "The soul who sins shall die. The son shall not bear the guilt of the father, nor the father shall bear the guilt of the son. The righteousness of the righteous shall be on himself, and the wickedness of the wicked shall be on himself."

That verse have always stuck with me because you're born in the world alone and you will leave alone, the world will not stop when you leave. Why waste time worrying about someone else's preservation for a prosperous live unless it's the family that you have. Then everyone else needs to worry, about the preservation for their lives. We grow at our own rate and what we need to do, is not go by how a flower grows faster than a tree and how an animal grows faster than a human.

By that logic, if we were to go by that mentality, we will forever desire to catch up to the growth of what is outside of us and not ourselves. That can be a dangerous thing. The tree grows at a slower rate than the flower, but it gets bigger, animals grows faster than the human. However, if you look at the growth of the opposition of the two, then you will realize that it, depends on what it's put into the growth. This determines how tall, how big, and how much growth will be needed according to the environment that it's in.

Thoughts of a prosperous life, races through the heads of those walking around daily. As we lay our heads down, we must wonder what will tomorrow bring.   What will be the next phase of my life? Will I succeed; will I fail in the attempts to put my family and myself in a higher position then where we were? Will the decisions, the actions that follow bring something wonderful to fruition or will they bring disaster to my life those that are around me? You must not worry about what tomorrow brings or the successes of failures that happen in your life. Life is the ultimate risk of the decisions and actions we make daily.

Chapter 3

180 Degrees

"We must realize that: everything that shines isn't gold, every sunny day isn't warm, and every flower isn't beautiful."

Predicting is in your Power

Life is like playing Russian Roulette. You'll keep spinning the chamber expecting the final click, which will end the circle of your life. That is why you must with strategic thought and precision, navigate through the school of life. With logic and forethought, we can be victorious and prosperous. We spend many days trying to predict our futures, either with tarot cards, psychic's or even with the so-called prophets of the many religions that are out there. So, we could see what our lives will be, if we know the path of the prosperous life that can be seen before we take the first step. Don't try to predict the future, by reading into the crystal ball of your own Jedi mind trick to see what your future holds. The only one that can predict the future, is the one that creates it.

What is the spark of the flame of your existence? What makes you want to wake up to live daily? What is the one thing you wouldn't dread doing? These are the questions you should ask yourself every day, that you sit in the quite place of your thoughts. What are your dreams, do you want to make them a reality? All it takes is the willingness to say, "anything will not stop or hold you back, to make the limited days on this Earth more pleasurable to live." Once you do that, then you will feel no stress, anxiety, worry, pain, or the constant unenviable desire to take on the feedback of those that say you can't do it.

Everyone has that beginning spark to live the prosperous existence. All you need, is to let Yes and No become your favorite words. The word YES is the spark of existence. When you have the thought and you manifest that in an actionable reality. You'll look back at the time that you were building yourself, into the experience of everything you built to get to that point, didn't exist until you said YES. The NO is also needed to tear down the walls of the false dichotomy that we have lived. When you say NO, you're saying, I will not be made into the fool that is your projection of me. No, I will live my life to the fullest. No, I will not walk on eggshells just to spare your feelings. I'm not dumbing myself down, just so you can feel better about the lack of intelligence that you have. When you give yourself the right to stand with those who society thinks is of a higher station, that is when you are becoming something far greater than you can ever imagine. You will be that much closer in coming FULL CIRCLE, with the very existence that have started the path to a wonderful life.

Eyes Wide Open

Wake up, the sun is shining, the sky is blue, the flowers are blooming, and the grass has that fresh cut smell. Breakfast is cooking, your drinking fresh squeezed orange juice, it's fresher than usual. Eggs are cooked to perfection, bacon is smelling good, it has the right crispiness and the toast isn't leaving crumbs in the butter. You are feeling yourself today. You have this invisible shield that protects you from the draconian system that you must live in. Nothing can touch you. Living the prosperous life and not having any worries, is like drinking cold water in 100-degree weather. You can feel the coolness in your chest, it is a feeling like no other. This is when you start to realize that the only way to feel like this, is not pushing your emotions down to spear feelings. However, it's to expose the mirror image to those that are within your circle and not holding anything back.

When you finally get to the point where something of anything doesn't bother you, then you're on your way to living the prosperous life that we all want. When you take care of your own physical, mental, emotion and spiritual health, you will be in full alignment and you will be one with everything that is good and bad in your life. You will have balance and not be on a half circle unbalanced existence. Balance is a good thing to have, especially when you're living the high life. Not the high life that gives you the materialistic mentality, but the high life of not have to think about if someone likes you. Also, not to put on airs for the next person, to belong into their circle. You can live the reality that you created, without being encumbered with the stories of how they tried at life and failed at the one task that they had to live the prosperous existence.

Put on your Glasses

I've talked about how to get to a prosperous existence and even how to live it. However, we get easily distracted by shiny things that really don't have anything to do with the task at hand. We get distracted by what shines and sparkles in the pretentious light of society. In hindsight, we think what is attracting us is healthy, but it is killing us slowly. We must always remember the one universal truth; that to live the life that is prosperous, pleasurable, peaceful and to walk with our heads held high. We must realize that everything that shines isn't gold, every sunny day isn't warm, and every flower isn't beautiful. However, you can be the sun that is warm, the flower that is beautiful and the gold that shines. Once you realize the power that is within you since the day you were born, you'll be unlimited in anything you do in life. Also, you will have the Midas touch of BLESSED BE's of everything in your path.

Same but Opposite Sides

The beginning is the end and the end is the beginning, which is a circle around the race of life. When we're born, live and die, we all leave an experience and go into another through the sands of time and changes. The lives we have, is just a drop a rain in the ocean. There will be many drops of rain, that with the ocean may flood over and cover the land that is you. However, as the puddles that are left behind, they go back into the sky through the process of evaporation. Also, the puddles go through changes from liquid to gas, it is a constant circle of life. When we look at it in this prospect, that is our lives in a nutshell. When we are born then a little bit of the ocean become the rain drop, when we leave this earth then the rain returns and become one with the ocean.

When you're in conflict with yourself, it is the worse life you can ever live, due to your whole being is wacked. Your decisions and actions will reflect the imbalance that you're living. Your conversations will be you repeating the same thing over and over, without any new subjects that would be of interest. You'll sleep for hours in a dark room because there's limited light that is coming from you. Also, you may be watching excessive amounts of tv just for an escape. Any kind of escape will be heaven, compare to the hell that you're living in, because of the imbalance of the scales, which is in the internal. The scales can go up or down depending which side you put the most weight on.

Balance of Scales

Talking about the balance of the ocean and the imbalance of the self-conflict, reminds me how when you have balance in your life, everything is copacetic. However, when you have an imbalance life, it will be a nightmare in the daytime. Negative and Positive is all around us, for those that says you can't have both or you need one or the other is incorrect. We need these 2 things for us not only to live, but to have balance. Think on it, have you ever seen a magnet stick to something without a negative and positive magnetic field, a car battery works with just a positive or a negative electrode. Also, no matter what anybody says, 2 positives and negatives never work with each other. This causes them to bounce back from each other, due only the opposite will attract. Also, have you ever seen an electron of an atom work without the proton and the neutron.   Not only there wouldn't be any balance with the nature that is around us, but there wouldn't be any balance with us.

2 Parts of a 3 Point Triangle

They're three points that we must recognize that is with us to have the triangular state of balance that is mind, body, and soul. If those are in line with each other, everything will be copacetic with you every day. However, even if one of those is off by even an inch, then you'll be walking with a lean. Your house is slightly off, with the loadbearing wall that is holding up your house, with a crumbling foundation that needs to be fixed. If the foundation of your house is gone, then your house falls. To strengthen your foundation, you must balance the land that the foundation is on. Repair the foundation, then buildup your house with the 3 loadbearing walls, which holds up the house of your serenity.

When I was thinking about the triangular state of mind, body, and soul. This was a revelation, it has everything to do with the FULL CIRCLE, in a way that, we are created as self-replicating organisms. The parents are the mind and body. Out of the mind and body, comes the child as a representation of the soul. The process of our creation is an infinite repeating process of the triangular states, which are born into existence. With this constant loop of creation, comes with the reruns of decisions and actions. The knowledge that we are in control of our actions, but we will always blame something else for what we do. The things we do daily starts out as a thought, then it manifests into an action that can affect the ability of how we as sentient beings navigate through the world. With the chain linked process of the triangular state and the FULL CIRCLE of mind, body, and soul.

Knocked Off

Most of the time, when we are not balanced with the three major points of balance, we are not thinking of the ways that we internalize everything we tell ourselves. Also, we allow outside influences to knock us off our balance. Your existence depends on how you treat and allow others to treat you in this plane of life. What you must realize, the way you treat your water of your soul does reflect on the outside. Water is formless, it has the greatest hold on memory. Sifu Bruce Lee said, "be like water, whatever you put water in it becomes what it's in, be formless and shapeless."

Listening to him say that while he was alive in an interview, he was right we must be formless and shapeless in all things. That is why you don't need to constantly put anything in your water that will keep you at a place of a dark abyss. Our bodies are 80% water and

everything we put into our "water", holds the memory of the last thing we've said or done. So,

we must be very aware of what we put in us, because what comes in can be held on to, all

depends on what you will put in and take out. Do you accept what you say about yourself, or

what others say about you? Do you accept the person that you are, or what others say you

are? Those questions need to be asked. There's one thing that we as a people are lacking, that

is the self-appreciating of who we are. Also, our ability to live according to how we look at

ourselves and not the image of someone else's prospective of who we are.

Yesterday's Trash

Another way of how we can live in the preverbal circle of our existence, is the way we

treat life on this plane of existence. It seems that, in this modern-day society, everybody is

worried about feelings and not be offensive to what others may think. Every time you think,

"why I'm on this plane of existence, what is my purpose. Why should I care, about what others

think about their views on you?" You need to come to the realization, that you are not alone in

those questions, that we must ask as a necessity for the answers we look for. Always

remember, life is 10 percent in what is in your reality and 90 percent how you react to the

situations that you come across daily.

The nonchalant way you should treat the issues that arise daily, is the greatest freedom

that you can have. When someone says, "I don't like you." Your reaction should be just like a

leaf in the wind, the farther it blows away from your presence, the sooner you can forget about it. When someone has an issue with you and you haven't done anything to that person, that is their perception of you and that is a personal issue that is within themselves. They need to take care of that. I remember when I was in school, this one person comes up to me, and told me, "I don't like anything about you." I've never done anything to this person, they were going by what someone else said about me. I said, "you don't even know me well enough to make that judgment," and I walked away. The way you should treat people's feelings about you when they say that they don't like you, is the same way you should treat a cup of coffee, when you throw the cup away, it's discarded never to be thought about again.

Blind Perception

Therefore, when someone says, "Perception is everything," I must look at them with a side eye. The way some use that saying, it's a cop-out so they can keep looking at you with what's in their minds. They don't realize the principle truth about that person, place, or thing.

I remember the first time I've ever eaten sushi; I've always thought that sushi was disgusting. The perception of eating raw fish, crab, and seaweed, didn't appeal to me as something that I would have bought as a first thought. My RA (Residential Advisor), was eating sushi rolls, I went to her office for something and I said, "ewww how can you eat that nasty stuff." She says to me, "have you ever tried sushi before," I said no. She gave me a piece of her sushi; it opened the flood gates, like Hannibal at the gates of the Roman Empire.

Telling that story hammers my point about Perception. You don't know what it is unless you have knowledge and understanding of the principle truth. Examples of how when you perceive people, place, and things, then you'll know the objective truth. What you think

something is, but you found that's not the truth, then Cognitive Dissonance kicks in. Case in

point; those who knew Ted Bundy, thought he was just an average guy who is a college student

who's good with the ladies. Except for those women that he killed in multiple states, then they

knew the truth of exactly who he was. Even when you meet a celebrity, you think they're the

same as you see on tv. In some cases, the role doesn't match the actor. Don't trust the

Perception of anything, always trust the truth and facts that can be proven.

Respect for the Reps

I've touched on this before in the earlier chapter about customer service and that I don't

like customer service. Due to, you must be phony while talking to these people, especially if

you're working for someone else's business where you can't be yourself. The person that they

tell you that, you must be nice so it's not to upset the customer. "The customer is always

right." Whoever came up with that saying, never once thought about the person who's on the

opposite side of that customer. Also, the internal fight that the customer service representative

must go through daily. So, they won't jeopardize their job or their dignity, by not giving in to

the anger, disgust, stress over someone else's issues. The constant want to verbally defend

yourself. Also, each of these companies tell you, "if someone curses you, is mean to you or they

just verbally berate you, DON'T TAKE IT PERSONALLY."   However, we as humans, with the

constant need to be balanced, can't help but to take that personally. Also, to take on the

customer's issues, is like getting mad at someone else because they're not paying their rent in

an apartment that's not yours. You shouldn't have to take on this issues or mistakes of the customer. That is their mistake, we need to be responsible for everything we do, not what someone else does.

I can't believe I forgot about the internal people who works at the same business you do. These are the people who make sure you're saying the right things, according to their standards. The "standards" that the company sets, these are the people who listen to your phone calls. Also, they score you, on how you fit in their company's way on how you handle these customers. Then again, how can they entrust a bunch of employees to score you on a job that they don't perform. Also, to work for a company that will just go their way and disregard any idea that wasn't theirs. Remember this, never entrust your livelihood to people who have no ambition outside that job. A J.O.B. is just something you use for at least 2 to 5 years, then either you get fired or you find another lily pad to land on.

I use the lily pad analogy to describe working for someone. Have you ever seen a frog hop on a lily pad, one after another until they get to solid ground? Have you noticed that, they don't sit on one for a long period of time? However, we're not smart like the frogs, we stay on the lily pad for too long. We don't feel ourselves sinking, so we think is safe to stay at a job or relationship for a long period of time. The pad will give out, because of the weight of your comfort is taking over your intellect. Don't sit on that pad for too long thinking that you have security when it is time to hop off do it. There have been people I've known who got comfortable eating at another person's table, while they're starving. Fix your own meals and sit at the head of your own table. When it is time, feast on your own fortune and not on the scraps of the so-called masters.

One day I received a call from a "customer" at my previous job Neiman Marcus Direct. I answered the phone with the usual greeting, "hello, thank you for calling my name is …… how may I help you." The "customer" said that we canceled her order and she wanted to know why. I said to her, "it is because we called you for 3 days in a row to get a form of payment and we never received a response, after 3 days the system cancels the order." She says, "how do we know that we called her," I said, "I was the one making the calls to your number." She never paid for her order. Also, she asked me the weirdest question, she asked, "are you jesus, I mean are you better than jesus." So, me being me said, "yes I'm better then jesus, because I exist, he doesn't." She was yelling at me and after telling her at least 3 times not to yell at me, she says to me, "man f**k you." It took everything inside me not to curse her out, so I hung up on her. That story hammers the point of constantly needing to hold on to the dignity that you have, so you can stand on your square and not get knocked off it by someone else's imaginary projection of who you are.

The Conscience Voice

That is why we have that little voice in our heads that pulls us back, when we're about to be outside of who we are. Listening to that inner voice is the seed that is the beginning of the growth for you to live the good life. This is the voice that everyone calls their conscious, needs to be heard, due to that is the part that is coming from the essence of your water. When you're listening to that voice what is it saying? Is the voice saying sweet things that vibrates your soul and raises the volume of your mind such as, "you're the most wonderful person alive, you're important, you're beautiful and smart no one can take that from you." Or, are you having darken fanatical thoughts of depression, envy, jealousy, anger? Also, are the voices constantly telling you, "you're worthless, your life isn't worth the person living it, every time you look in the mirror, you see a loser?" When the voices tells you these things just remember, YOU'RE the source of this voice. Also, the source of the negative and positive activities in your life.

You have 2 ears and 1 mouth. When these dark and light thoughts come from your internal energy that is your essence. They manifest from your energy, from there to your mouth, then to your ears. This is the continuous cycle of thoughts, speaking and hearing. We must be on the lookout from when it starts to affect us not only physically, but also mentally and spiritually. Remember what the lesson is in the scriptural context, "do not conform to the world, but be transformed by the renewal of YOUR mind." That is how you'll have the ability to move along in the evolution of your existence.

When it comes to telling yourself positive things, especially when life don't go exactly how you have planned or wanted. Our lot in life, we must take the good with the evil. To know the storm and the sunshine, the winter with the summer, death with life and the up and down. In my experience, when you are the one hearing and being on the end of life's disappointments. You can be mad about it, have your time to express your feelings about the disappointment and after you finish being angry, then say these 2 words, "OH WELL". Those 2 words are the catalyst of not allowing the bullshit to get to you. Also, not allowing someone outside of you to bring down the tranquility that you have accomplished. Always put this in your mind: never allow anybody to extinguish the flame that you have started. Also, don't ever let anybody change who you are or the advantageous lifestyle that you can accomplish.

I remember as a teenager, I've always heard people say, "you can't do this or that," or "if I couldn't do it, I know you can't either." You must constantly remind the people that say those things, that you are not them and if they couldn't do something that's on them. That person who thinks they accomplished peace in their lives, your mirror is the reflection of that other person's inadequacies. When they point out that your less than they are, they're projecting how they feel on the inside onto you. With that projection of themselves on you, it is an anathema to your existence. When you allow it to affect you to the point of being in a mental frozen state, thaw yourself from the cold of their projections. Also, have the warm embrace of your own identity.

Patience is a Seed

In this life as I'm getting older, I've learned not to allow anything in this present time to affect my future. How you live, your actions dictate what kind of future you will have. When you make plans, remember this: plans can change at the drop of a dime. So, it will behoove you not to put so much stock in someone else making plans for you and tell you what the outcome of your future will be. Once you wake up from the slumber of your issues that plague your existence. Plans will be set in motion for you to live your best life without the issues. However, it will be up to you to guide those plans and see them to fruition. When your plans come into fruition and it is exactly how you planned, take a step back and thank yourself for not allowing someone else's hesitant actions affect your life.

I was talking to my other half a couple of days ago, she always ask the same question; "when will it be my time, why do I have to be patient?" I said that her time is coming for her to be in a place that she wants to be. Have you ever asked yourself when is the time? When is the day, when is the year of this tangible reality that we are in, that I will be in the place that I want to be? As you ask yourself these questions, remember what was said in the earlier chapters about time. The realization that when the seconds, minutes, hours, days, weeks, months, and years pass, you can never go back to that time. That is why we should make every second count towards striving, rising above the bitter taste of losing battles and relishing the victory of your war.

We all have things in our lives that we go through daily, the one thing for those of us who have unresolved issues with society, family, friends and our significant others must do, is find the catalysis of these issues and put out the spark before the fire of the antiquated time line reaches the gasoline of the future of your path of peace. When you light the way for your peace, remember this: don't let the fire of your desire be put out by the extinguishing acts of those that don't want to see you rise. Always check the circle that you build. So, it won't become a dot of mistrust, greed, jealousy, and envy. When it comes to the rising of you reaching the top of the mountain of your existence. This is the part in which you don't want to put to memory. So, not to crack open your head, only to spill out the memories that will only put you back to the beginning. Also, not to internalize, you would only want to filter out the dark from the light.

The Quiet Place

There's a saying that I came up with while I was in my thoughts in the quiet place. The saying goes like this, "be careful of the person wearing a blind fold with the eye's cutout." That saying speaks volumes, to the personalities of those who can look at everybody else and what their issues are. However, can't look at themselves and know that they have issues, they need to look at the reflective mirror of life. For you, to be blind of the life experiences that you have lived but can point out the issues in someone else's existence. You're on a one-way journey, to the hypocritical abyss void of the universe that is you. It is the abyss of emptiness in their mind state. When they catch the cold of the draconian society, in the tangible existence that they internalize, as a misfortune of their own doing.

Always Remember the Golden Rule of the scriptural context, "don't look at the plank in someone else's eye, when you can't see the dirt in yours." When you understand that you must look at yourself when you make mistakes but careful not admonish someone when they have missteps in life. We all have knowledge when we do something wrong, especially when we were younger. However, we always seem to forget when we didn't have the knowledge, in order not to make the mistakes that we made. The decisions that led us to a place of paying for the hard lessons that we learned along the way. Once you can see what the mirror of your own reflection is, only then you can move to the next evolution of your circle that is the growing plant that is you.

Existence is Proof

Never forget those lessons that you have learned from the mistakes we have done and will still do. Every day is a learning experience, not one of us on this earth have ALL the knowledge of this world or the universe. It's ok just to say, "I don't know." Don't make it up as you go and say something that you can't prove the existence of did it.

Earlier it was said that balance and the desire for it is needed to live this life. Also, the way that we need to have those things, so we can live our best lives. When I think about the things that we need to have balance and not allowing someone else's unbalance to knock you off your square.

I think of fire, how it burns and is never extinguished. Except, when someone puts the fire out, so it won't burn or keep you warm when the world is cold to you. Remember this: the fire can never be extinguished by pouring the gasoline of your desire for better things. As a wise man named Kevin W'esly said, "a candle can never be dimmed by lighting another one." Keep the fires of your desire burning, light the candles along the way. Also, never forget the beginning of the fire burning, the candles lit, is the spark of the flicker of your lighter.

Chapter 4

240 Degrees

"It's not what people call you, it's not even what you answer to, it's what you accept."

It's only half of the Story

"Remember, you would want to do a 180 degree turn for the changes that are possible for your life". That was said to me at a young age. Those words resonated with me as if it was the gospel truth and the person who said it was a savior. It wasn't until I was going through the ages of time, I found out with years of researching, understanding, meditating, and going in the rabbit holes to see how deep it can go. That the 180-degree turn will leave you at an imbalance. This is an example that you may think that you have the full knowledge of a subject. However, when you were doing the Absent-Minded Professor research, you found out that what you thought you knew wasn't the entirety of the knowledge, it is only that you know.

As above so is below, sounds familiar? You've heard this before in the churches but said like this, "as in Heaven so is on Earth." It means the same thing. Both of those sayings hammers the point of, when you look at the cycles of life in that aspect, you will soon realize that the 180 degrees of the circle of your existence is a missing part of the whole story. Which is the full rotation of your essence. When the earth rotates on the axis of its space, you see the daylight rise, and the night to come only for the day to start again. However, if the 180 degrees philosophy was true, then it would be forever night on one side of the world and light on the other. When that happens, the whole world is unbalanced and chaotic.

Therefore, everybody must look at the entirety of everything not just the dogmatic view of what you were taught. The 360 degrees is the way to have balance of the chaotic world that is within the essence of your whole being of your existence. A circle has no corners, which is the limited space that we must go around, only to come across another limited space. We

mustn't limit ourselves to the corners of this life, we need to be limitless in the possibilities of

this existence, never put yourself in a box of labels, professions, lifestyles, and reaching of what

you want out of life.

Everything that we see daily has a full circle of existence, such as planets, humans,

animals. Plants are planted with the seeds of their beginnings and humans are born, so will

they go through the rotations of life. Each of these things go through a separation of the

experiences that they will live and have new beginnings. This is the circle of lives that we live,

the people we love, and the things that we have learned. Every being on this earth is a self-

replicating organism, and as these self-replicating organisms, on a consistent basis we have new

beginnings daily and new circle of lives to start.

You don't Know

The cycle of the existence of these intricacies, is the matter of what we perceive at the

levels of our comprehension of the miscegenation of our experiences that we comment to daily.

We come across the mixture of our experiences daily in the world, the people that you may

think that they don't understand what you're going through, but you'll be surprised of the

people that is going through the same thing as you. "You don't understand what I'm going

through", I've heard that many times and some instances that is true, I'll never understand

what it means to be a single mother, a drug addict, an alcoholic, or someone that is constantly

living with the Murphy's Law syndrome. That being said they're people who are in this world who knows EXACTLY how it is to be unfulfilled living a life of mediocracy, who's family isn't what you want them to be, knowing you're just as intelligent as the next person but you don't have a start to show yourself and the world that you are important. All the answers to your life it all starts with the person that you have to face in the mirror and while you're looking in the mirror and wonder to yourself, "will anyone accept me for who I am and not what they want me to be", well don't wonder what anyone else will accept, but only what you will accept of yourself.

Curses of a Generation

I spoke about in the earlier pages about when I was going to church when I was younger, and I used to hear about this issue among the members and the clergy alike, it was about Generational Curses. Have you ever heard about these Generational Curses maybe in passing conversations, well I'm pretty sure that even if you never heard of that term, you have seen it in real life maybe in your family or someone else's? These so-called curses have put people in a position of not being able to get over that hump of not be successful in their lives because of this hold. These so-called curses could have been a family member from days pass that could have done something, lived a lifestyle that wasn't in their best interest or had a mental diagnosis that was other than sane.

These so-called curses are only in the circle of the family structure due to, not one person in the future generation didn't break the chain of the circle of poverty, hatred, having no moral compass, drug abuse, and alcoholism. The curses are going around the infinite structure that is their existence. This is the part of your cycle of the familial circle of the new generation that can break this cycle of events, and start a new circle that gets rid of these so-called curses that ruined the past generation and the Sir Isaac Newton, "for every action, there's an equal and opposite reaction", relation of the curse that started with one member of your family. To be honest to the readers of this book, I personally don't believe that one person in a family can start a chain of events that determine what a person who is not them, can follow the same path as the person who started that circle, when everybody who have the knowledge and forethought to follow their own path that they forged themselves.

Speaking about the so-called Generational Curses, I was watching a documentary about the infamous serial killer Theodore "Ted" Bundy, it was about his confession tapes that was made with him during his murder trials. Little did I know that he had a daughter with his wife when she was visiting him while he was in jail in Florida, I guess they must have had some "alone" time and the guards were busy with another prisoner's hint. If these so-called Generational Curses had some truth in it, then why isn't his daughter a serial killer, or living a life full of strife knowing that you're the descendant of a serial killer. The only Generational Curse that is true is the one you'll put on yourself if you make decisions and commit actions that will put you in a place of constantly mistaking the difference of just existing or living a life that you don't have to be stressed over.

In the degrees of the circle of your existence, the life you want can be accomplished through the observations of your past, right along with the stacking of your present, to the FULL CIRCLE that is your future. Once you accomplish the starting of the continuous circle of a new existence. You'll have peace within knowing you broke that circle of past uncertainty of the question; will anything from my past effect my accomplishments in my future? You can't allow the past events that went on in your family, to affect what you must do to have the stability you long for. When you allow your stability to turn into instability, then you're not on your square and you'll become an easy target for manipulative people.

Gems Droppin'

When I was younger, I watched this show called Quantum Leap, this was my favorite show because it did drop some gems with each episode and the fact it was talking about spiritual reincarnation. Sam, the character on the show, when he leaped into a person, he knew he was himself but when we looked in the mirror it was the person that he leaped into, he couldn't leave that body without completing the task that he was there for. That was an example of how life and death should be. We're here for our life and the growth of it, not to plant your seed in another field that doesn't have a potential for harvest.

In the earlier chapter, I was speaking about how time passes to never to be returned to the previous, and how the Earth goes in one direction, so does the physical measurement of time. As I'm writing this book the time is 12:29pm on May 23, 2019, in 60 seconds it will be 12:30pm, as fast as it took for the time to change the past has already left you. Once that happens, the past is now a void of empty spaces and a trail of memories that where left behind, like the rapture of your spirit that flees from your body when your time is up.

Tick tock, tick tock, snap your fingers, clap your hands together. The speed of these things that takes seconds to do, is also the seconds it takes for you to not hold on to the thoughts, decisions and actions that would make you have that void of the life that you have built up. As I said in the earlier chapters, "what took years to build can be destroyed in seconds." In this cycle is one in which we must not hold on to the problems, frustrations, and anger of what was once there. Now gone in the extinction, of the animalistic view that you left in the rearview mirror of your life. When you no longer have these things that put you in the state of mind of there's no end to the issues, only then you can move on to the next evolution of the circle of life.

The advancement of your existence depends on what has taken place, what is taking place and what will take place in the future. There's a starting point in the circle of your life, and it all begins with the strike of the match and the lighting of the dynamite that is your beginning. When the dynamite of life is lit, you will go through a series of events that will determine your successes or your so-called failures. Once you have the knowledge, wisdom and overstanding of what needs to happen, you can transform into the being that you are meant to be. Not the supposed norm of the societal need, to take you out of your circle and put you in a box of limitations.

Limitations is only real if you make it real. I remember I was reading a book from the Star Wars canon called Darth Bane: Path of Destruction. Darth Bane was fed up with the limitations that the Sith organization was putting on him, not to look at the Sith records of those that were before him. He thirsted for the knowledge that they had, to be the ultimate power in the Sith organization. Also, to be the strongest connected to the dark side of the Force. That's how you keep going, always seek answers to life's questions and achieve great things that will take you out of your comfort zone of mediocracy. Also remember this: never

accept shallow knowledge, and think you have all of it. You can have all the degrees in the

world, study all the world's religions, and still not have all the knowledge that you look for.

Greek philosophers such as Homer, Socrates, and Aesop, constantly sought knowledge from the

teachers they were under. Even as philosophers and educated men, they still didn't have all the

knowledge, it was always a thirst for more.

In the advancement of this phase of your circle, you must remember this saying, "it's not

what people call you, it's not even what you answer to, it is what you accept." If you accept the

limitations of what others that are not part of your infinite circle label you, then you become

the perpetrator of the circumstance that someone else has brought into your life. I was

conversing with my co-worker just 2 weeks ago and we were just talking about labels and life. I

shared that the way I speak about things such as current events involving, manufactured

phobias, millennial safe spaces, and religion. I was telling her the way I speak about religion to

those on the outside looking in, people would think that I were an Atheist. I was telling her

about the time I was doing a live video speaking about religion, someone called me an Atheist. I

told that person that I'm not one and they were trying to put that label on me. Therefore, you

must get yourself out of the Matrix of labels, so no one can even try to put their labels on you,

and that you must accept them.

The perpetuation of labels and what others put on you can't be tolerated or allowed in

your circle. As a sentient being that can think, feel, touch, taste, smell and see. You must not

allow the meteor of someone else's projected incapability's, to knock off the axis of the planet that is within your solar system. Without labels everybody is naked, every one of us are wearing the Emperor's New Clothes. We think we have some fine threads, that we are showing off, that's a projection of your mind due to these labels. Also, just like the Emperors clothes, we are making fools out of ourselves to put ourselves higher than the next person. Especially, when all the while we forget, that one day when the smoke clears and when it is all said a done, the labels will be all for nothing. What's the difference between the graveyard of a CEO of a company and the janitor? The ashes of King and the subject? The difference is the funeral plans that those who they left behind make to bury or cremate them.

Titles Don't mean Shhhhhhhhhh

"I'm a nurse, I'm a doctor, I'm the Chairman of my corporation." All these titles are nothing, but the regurgitation of those who use these titles to put themselves above you as saying, "I'm superior because the society that I live in told me so." I remember at the job I'm working at, there were these representatives from a company. They had these nurses that worked for them, they had the arrogance of a know-it-all, using their position to put themselves above those who they speak to. There's a saying that I have; "arrogance is an illusion, especially when someone else is signing your paychecks." These are what labels and titles can do for a person who is too weak minded to know that, the way you got that title, is the same way you can lose it.

No matter the accomplishments you perform, the awards you receive, the religions that you are in and the titles of the followers of those religions, it will all be for naught. The reason why it will all be for naught, is due to these are physical things never to be taken with you and they will stay on the Earth when you leave. I forgot this part of the question from the earlier paragraph. What's the difference between the religious and the Atheist? Nothing, those are just labels that either were given, taught, or accepted. Everything that you ever disagreed with, the same way you were taught it, you can dismiss it just the same. You must never be bogged down with the constant acceptance of labels, that you have been given. So humble yourself, otherwise you will soon discover the universal truth, that is no matter what title you have, it can be taken away and someone else will take your place. The title will always be there, but you won't be. You're not the title, you're just the person filling a position.

"People will always look for an advantage from those who they perceive as weak." Saying that makes me thing of the story of the Tortoise and the Hare, the Hare challenged the Tortoise to see who will win the race. The Hare had the advantage of speed and the Hare thought that the Tortoise will be an easy win due to the Tortoise is slow. They started the race and the Hare took off as fast as he could, passing up the Tortoise while he is going at his own pace. At the end of the race, it wasn't the one who were the fastest who won the race, it was the one who took their time to analyze that path that was in front of him.

The lesson that can be taken from that story is this: on the path of the cycle of your existence, you can't race to the finish line based on someone else's speed, you have to go with the pace that matches the revolution of the start of the race in your life. In society we have people that try to race pass the person, who they conjured a competition within their minds. Those are the people who are so far behind in the race, they think they're winning. Also remember this the start and finish are at the same point but on the opposite sides of the line by an inch that is between them, this is a chasm seems so close but far away from the goal. I remember when I was in high school, we had to run the 800-yard dash as an assignment on the track. We started the race and I was running, reached halfway but I started to get tired, I thought I couldn't finish but I made it to the finish line and received a passing grade. As I'm sitting here writing this book, I'm thinking about that time and just like the tortoise I was slow and steady and finished the race. In the earlier pages, it was discussed that, when someone says, the 180-degree turn is the point that you need to make a change for the better. To hammer my point of how that logic is flawed; to make a complete change of not only the way you look at the tangible existence that is in front of you but also the way you react to it as well.

2 Halves make a whole One

We always would think that the 360 degree is back where you started, and the 180-degree change is good. However, if everything that is a living organism including the planet you live on had that kind of logic. On one side of the world, it would never be daylight ever again. Everything would wither and die. Also, the other side would forever be daylight, everything would burn. Every human on this Earth and most animals came together to create one of the species that they belong to. Not one human or birthing mammals has ever been created with just one half of the species without its counterpart. Our mothers and fathers came to together with each other's consent, to create one or more children, either male or female. Depending which chromosome, we received that determines the sex, which means we're half our mothers and fathers, we became one being.

The balance is not something that is outside of us, it has always been within our essence that is us. This is also the reason that you must look within for the balance that is on the scales of the thoughts, choices and actions that follow you daily. That can determine which side of the scales that can be pinpointed. Will the scales be weighted the same on both sides, or will you feed the wolf that can tilt the weight of the imbalance of the inner pounds? That is the unfinished product of the missing ingredients of the fallen cake.

We're Still Children

One day I was conversing with a friend of mine, she asked me a very interesting question, "do you think that we as men and women act like children?" Here is what I told her, "in the aspect of 'acting like children.' Is it that we act like children or are we regressing back to the memory and actions of when we were young?" I say that we do sometimes go back to the memories that when we didn't get our way with what we wanted. We throw temper tantrums and get mad at the person who told us no about something, throw things, show off our toys that we got, go steady. However, now they call it hooking up or hanging out and playing video games."

There are people in the world who knowingly or unknowingly transfer the time of when they were children into becoming an adult. We would like to think that we as humans are well balanced and that all we must do is live the life that was set in front of us. Unfortunately, that is not always the case. The things we do daily can be derailed by the unbalanced childlike tantrums, which were transferred from the lack of repair of the issues that as a child we went through. Once this happens, the transference of the child like behavior, has now came into the incomplete circle of adulthood.

We must be balanced at the start as children, so we won't damage the world with the behaviors that we used to be punished for when we throw our fits of unrepaired rage. We must cut the umbilical cord of the mother of the unseen issues that will affect the tangible relationships that we involve ourselves in daily. The way we must escape the prison of being childlike in the negativity, is when you think about growing into the fullness of adulthood, you should remember the scriptural aspect of this saying: "when I was a child, I spoke as a child, I did things as a child, I understood as a child, but when I became a man I put away childish things". What we must do is put away the toys of the unbalanced pass into the chest of the present, so you can move forward into the balanced future. The one you will create, with an advanced ability to react to any situation that you will come across.

We Distract Ourselves

I take the train daily to my job. When I ride the train, I notice everyone looks down on their phones. For the reasons of getting the latest gossip, who's on Facebook or what other distractions they may be into. Every now and again we need to look up from the distractions that we hold on to in our hands, these are called distractions for a reason. The word DISTRACTION comes from the Latin word "distractionem" meaning, "a pulling apart, separating," also from the stem "distrahere," meaning, "mental disturbance." So, when you think about the word DISTRACTION, it means you're giving your attention to something that is without purpose. This can be an issue, when you give your attention to things and situations that doesn't help you strive in this circle of life. Once you open your eyes to these distractions that are not only around you, but also the ones you put yourself in, then you can potentially live your life free of issues that will not allow you to prosper.

"You will reap what you sow" or "what goes around will come around." You heard that before, but have you ever thought about what those 2 sayings really meant? Does it mean that, if you plant a seed it grows, then you can harvest it? Or does it mean, whatever you plant in the karmatic universe you will harvest what comes from it? The latter of those two questions is the answer that is a testament of the Boomerang Effect, which happens when you put out the energy that comes back to you.

Chapter 5

300 Degrees

"Good can't survive without evil, dark can't exist without light and love can't survive without hate."

When you Throw, it will Comeback

I've been a witness of the Boomerang Effect of the karmatic justice that was planted in the ground of the self-universe that is us. I remember this like it was yesterday, back when I was in high school, I used to go to church with my cousin when we lived in Illinois. There was this woman, we'll call her "M." Her husband and she were members of the church I attended; they were members of that church at that time 5 years before I came. On the outside looking in I thought they had it together, he had a good job I think it was at a local tv station and she was a secretary at that time. They were godparents to this young lady at the time, we'll call her "P," she's a couple of years younger than me I was 16 at that time. Now I have been going to that church for a year, I turned 17 while going to that church and we would do outings.

One day, "M's" husband and her invited me over to their house with "P" to watch movies and eat dinner. We watch Rumble in the Bronx, the Jackie Chan movie, I digress, while we were eating and conversing at the dinner table. "M," when no one was looking, started blowing kisses at me. At first, I laughed it off due to in my mind I thought she was joking, then something in my mind finally clicked, I came to the realization that what she was doing wasn't a laughing matter and she not joking. My psyche at that time, couldn't understand why she were doing this when her husband was just in the living room.

The next time I seen her, she pulled me to the side, she said, "I was just playing with you and I hope you didn't take it the wrong way", I said, "it's cool I can take a joke". From then I put it out of my thoughts, but now as I'm telling this story, I knew in the back of my mind that she wasn't joking, I let it pass but nothing prepared me from what happened next. One day on February 18th, 1998, I remember this date due to how cold it was that year and it was a school night. I was watching tv in my living room and I heard a knock at the door, I looked out of the window through the blinds, it was "M."

I opened the door, she said, "are you busy," I said no, the she said, "come on get dressed we have somewhere to go." I figured it was one of our church outings again, I got dressed and went with her. We went to this park over in DP, it was across the bridge from where I lived at. She parked the car, turned the car off and I'm wondering why are we at this park, in the winter, 15-degree weather with snow on the ground. She says, "I heard something about you," I'm wondering what she heard, I asked her, "what did you hear about me." I'm thinking she was going to say that her goddaughter had a crush on me or something to that affect. What she said next shocked the hell out of me. She says to me, "I hear that you like me as a woman" (meaning that I wanted to have a relationship with her). Now at this time she's 10 years older than me, also she got a whole husband at home, but she kept saying to me, "I can get I trouble, you're too young for me to have a relationship with". She kept repeating that to me and not one time did she ever mention the MAJOR reason why we couldn't have a relationship even if I were old enough, is that she MARRIED!

All my life I never feared anyone of the opposite sex, I guess that's how I knew that women would be a major part of my life, wink, but I digress. I had a girlfriend at the time, my best friend is a female, so I never had a reason to be scared, until that day. I said to her, "I never said that, also I would never have a relationship with her because she is married. She started the car and started driving back to my house, I was silent for most of the trip, she was trying to make small talk, I really wasn't up for talking, well at least to her. Then she said this to me, "what if I wanted to start a relationship with you how would you feel about that," I didn't give an answer.

She dropped me off and drive away, I was only gone for an hour, but it felt like years. The next Sunday I seen her at church, she came to me and said, "I apologize about the other night." This time I kept the events of that night in the front of my mind, also didn't forget about that date to this day. I stop going to that church, my cousin informed me that M's husband filed for a divorce. He found out what she was trying to do, to this day I don't even know how he found out. I never told anybody in that church what she did, I also found out that I wasn't the only one, he meet another woman and moved out. The next I saw her, she didn't look very well, it looked like life got the best of her. However, it wasn't life, it was the seeds she planted to change the course of events in her life coming to harvest.

The next story of the Boomerang Effect is about someone I knew but this time I was a witness. We'll call her "L," well L was a wonderful woman, she worked hard, she was raising her children to the best of her ability, however she was the perpetrating catalyst of the gasoline that was thrown on the fire that was already burning. She had a relationship with a man, we'll call him "A." At first, she was happy that they were together, they went out on dates, he came over for dinner, they did everything together. There's one issue, he was married, she knew that he was married but she didn't care. She said that same tired line that every woman who deals with married men say, "if he was happy at home, he wouldn't come to me." Almost a year later A's wife found out about the affair, she divorced him, the woman that he was seeing said that she didn't want to see him again, he lost his house, car, and job in less than a year.

L got married 2 years later after the events of her affair with A. We all know the boomerang of the karmic justice doesn't have an end date; L's husband had an affair with another woman. The other woman was saying the same thing that L said when she was with that married man. She was heartbroken, then a light clicked on, she came to the realization that the same thing is happening to her, that woman was a relative of mine. These stories were told not to put someone in a bad light, but to say that in the circle of existence, we must remember, what you put out the boomerang will go back to the source of the one who threw it.

Things happen for a reason, 9 times out of 10 we're that reason that things happen in our lives. We must understand that in the universal circle of existence in these situations, whatever you put out, you will get back. The infinite circle keeps going around and around, until you make a circle of a new beginning. That will be free of the weeds you planted, so the garden of your life will blossom. If you're not able to pluck those weeds of self-doubt and use the intellect that you know you have, to put yourself in a position of being successful in your life. Also, not to use the very same intellect that you must make your own choices, then you don't deserve sympathy, if your life isn't going the way you want it to go. Also, you are not attempting to make any changes but complaining about the details of your life.

Sun behind a Dark Universe

Have you ever looked up at night and wondered, can light and dark coincide each other? Also, look at couples and say to yourself, "is it a constant back and forth of their love/hate or are they a balanced compromise?" The reason these questions are asked is because one can't survive without the other. Good can't survive without evil, dark can't exist without light and love can't survive without hate. All through history there have been civilizations older than any modern-day religious beliefs who got this concept, such as in the African Spiritual practice Vodun. It was believed, there were multiple Divine principals who at one time were on this planet that are watching them. In Kemet (modern day Egypt), they believed in Divine principals as well. Also, they believed that men and women were spiritually connected as masculine and feminine. They also believed in the 142 laws of Ma'at (where the 10 commandments came from). They believed that all things were scared and shared the same energy. These 2 spiritual systems also shared the common belief when it came to good/evil, and light/dark. They couldn't survive without each other. Also, to go with one or the other would bring you at an imbalance.

This is where the modern-day religious institutions get it wrong, such as Christianity. Christianity, (including Catholics), believe that their god and devil are enemies. The whole reason why the so-called devil and this god are enemies, this devil said that "he" wanted his own kingdom. "Him" and one-third of "his" followers where casted out. "He," made the so-called first humans on Earth sin. The only way that humanity could be saved, is by sending this gods son on earth to atone for the so-called sins of others. The question is, "why couldn't this god just kill the devil and eliminate evil?" Could you kill something that is part of yourself, part of a whole package that makes us who we are? If you don't know the answer to that question, then you don't know who you really are.

They're more questions than answers these days. Will I go left or right in the evolution of my decisions and the actions that follow for the rest of my life? Will I go up to the limitless sky or will I go down to the ground of the misery of limits? As you sit and wonder about the opposite sides of the same coin of life think about this; when you look at the spectrum of things that went on in your life, did you see love turn into hate, good turned into evil, dark become light? With these events that you saw, did you go through them yourself or were you a witness to these situations? Love can circle into hate at the drop of a dime. It could be something that happened with you, a loved one or when you were younger you had an issue with a person, place, and thing.

The love you may had for that person, turned into hate because they were with someone behind your back. Also, they burned the bridge of your love, life, and loyalty that you gave them as an overflowing cup of your soul. Love and hate are powerful feelings, actions that intertwine in the infinite circle of existence. These 2 actions can be changed as night and day, into the figure 8 of colliding planets into one mass and move simultaneously in a full circle rotation. Love/hate are depended upon how the turns of the circle rotates daily until the rotation stops. Then you will find that the nature of things that you had hate for, now you look at with complete adoration of bursting appreciation of love.

In your life, you must find inside yourself the things you love/hate, what you will keep and what you will not. Love and hate is not a terrible thing, especially when a habit that you love is killing you slowly such as smoking cigarettes, being in a relationship that is not helping you grow or being surrounded by people who don't have your best interest at hand. You must learn to hate the things that dims you daily, that is a part of your existence. Love what brings you peace and tranquility, hate what brings chaos.

Darkness and Light is of the same circle of your existence. They coexist as a circular balance, on opposite sides of the coin that flips in the decisions of the actions that you do daily. Remember in the earlier pages it was mentioned that religions got it wrong when it came to dark and light. In the modern-day religions, we were told that darkness and light wouldn't be able to co-exist and you must choose one side. This is not true. Just like the 180-degree philosophy that was spoken of in the previous pages, you can't have one without the other you would have an imbalance. You will be leaned over without the weight of the other side of the scale, to balance the equal sided circle of existence of dark and light. An example of dark and light existing together, is the universe has many sources of light in the background of darkness. To illuminate as the balance of the universal coexistence of dark and light.

In many stories of religious text, dark and light is always in a constant battle with each other, with us to pick the side that feeds into our sensibilities. That would be the wrong to do, we can't pick sides of something that is the very core of who we are. We must be the electron of the positive and negative representation of dark and light to have balance, so we don't lean to one side or the other. We can fall into despair of having an imbalance of the circle that is you. You will only know of the 180 degrees and not multiply it by 2. This would only allow you to bring half of your potential to the table to never be fully satisfied. The existence of dark and light is something that we go through. Whether you're in your feelings, your ability to forgive those who did you wrong, to let go of the bitter taste of never achieving your objective for what you perceive as a better life or the reflection of the self-hatred in the mirror. Dark and light was never to fight against each other, they were always supposed to intertwine into one. When you understand that, you will understand how to be balanced in this phase in your life.

Duality of Essence

Remember in the earlier pages that it was spoken about As Above as Below, that goes into the up and down in the circle of existence. When you look up in the and say, "what's that," you see the night sky, you may think you're looking at the void that is outer space. However, what we're not realizing is that what you're looking at, is the foundation of the essence that you were born with. The up and down is part of the circular balance of your existence, which is the start and finish of the elevator that is life. It can go up and down as the buttons is pushed to the floors of the stages of life, that's manifested in the building of the triangular mind, body, and soul of you. When you think about the up and downs in life, we must look at all sides of the above and below of the life that you live daily, to realize that we must embrace this part of the circle. So, we're not blind in the fairy tales of roses and blue skies all the time, but in the reality of things. So, we can be a better version of ourselves daily.

Each person in the world, go through a full circle of events daily. The circle is the shift of events in a linear time, which is part of the tangible existence we live in. This is comparable to working difference shifts at a job to keep at business running. Each person who work those shifts, are part of the joint effort for that business to function. This happens daily in a constant circle. If this circle brakes due to the business, it begins a change. Cutting the supply and demand of the employees that kept your company afloat, a customer service 1-star reputation, this circle will cease to exist. Understand that in this part of the circle, everything is connected in the transference of energy. That includes the economics that drive the society of bartering that makes the world go around. Each of us use this to move throughout the world, at different levels of the businesses that are present. Everyone has their place in this circle to distribute goods and services, which are part of our daily lives. This circle can't be disturbed, if one part of this foundational pillar fall, then the whole house of your circle will crumble. Also, the wreckage that is left behind is the downfall of the foundation, which is the load bearing wall that was kicked from under the foot of the dream that turned into a nightmare.

Remember the Merry-go-Round in the park, when it was spun around it kept going around, it did not stop until someone stopped it or slowed down enough to jump off? That is exactly how life is, the constant around, around it goes and when will stop no one knows. Except, the marry-go-around of your life it keeps going, even when you attempt to slow it down or jump off when you no longer want to go through the motions of being a stranger in the sea of lives that are lived daily. Never stop the marry-go-round, it is the truth of the example of how life is and the circle of the ideas, possibilities, and uniqueness of changes that we go through. Remember the circle goes forward and never backwards, due to going backwards is a

block of the forward time that you will experience. The merry-go-round looks funny going

backwards. However, in the society we are living in, the ride that always moves forward is

starting to do the unnatural act of going in reverse.

Chapter 6

360 Degrees

(The Complete Circle)

"The philosophy of the Full Circle comes down to the 6 points of life, which need to be lived by. They are: Life, Love, Loyalty, Knowledge, Wisdom and Understanding."

Ass Backwards

The fly captures the spider in its web, the Gazelle hunts the lion and the lion is prey. The hyena is the King of the jungle, the sky is the ground, a lie is the truth and the truth is a lie. These are a shock to the system of the forward moving linear time of existence. The circle must move forward to have perfect balance. To put the puzzle together, with the pieces that can fit together for the completed picture of the live that you could live. Once you have the balance of the merry-go-round spinning in the correct direction of the existence of you mind, body and soul, then you will be able to move through the sea of time without the anchor of instability.

Different Soil

I remember a conversation that I had with my mother one time, she reminded me of something. She reminded me of when she was younger, her mother couldn't read and write. She taught herself how to read and write. When I was thinking about that, I could not help but to think that we came from a family of people of persevered in conditions that were unfavorable. My grandmother to me was the start of the circle of family members who planted their own seed in locations that were far from their origin. Everyone in my family started their own circles, with each member of the family we have started, some of us are in the middle and the rest have completed their circle.

This is the circle of family passing on generation of traits, traditions, and stories. With each circle, comes along new traditions added to the already written story of life the ones before you have lived. The story of the pages is the continuous circle of stories, which have been told and will keep being told with added pages until the last page is completed. This is part of the circle that is the continuous chain of events, which goes on in every family across the world. Just like dirt from the United States to Mexico, the sands from the beaches of Hawaii to the coast of Africa, there isn't any difference of the start and finish of the stories that we pass on. That is what makes us part of the same world and the descendants of the universal circle of life, energies, and the beginning of all things. Born into existence to finish their chapters of their full circle resurrection.

Natural Transformation

In this society, we make things up to justify the rose-colored view that we have or how things we think should be. However, not the principle of what it is to solidify the truth of things. We have made up definitions for ourselves; phobias, and labels to now be all-inclusive to these supposed struggles. This was touched on in the earlier pages but didn't go in-depth. Such manufactured phobias are the ones that has to do with those who went through transformations that are not on the natural side of nature. Merriam-Webster defines Transformation as: "an act, process, or instance of transforming or being transformed." A caterpillar into a Butterfly, a maggot into a fly, a child into an adult and young to old. These are transformations that happen in nature.

Also, Merriam-Webster defines Phobia as: "an ill rational fear or a strong dislike for someone or something." When you put those 2 words together, you're really saying that, you are afraid or dislike things that go through natural transformations. That translation is being used to say; if a person does not accept an unnatural transformation, they're looked upon as evil or non-progressive. To the point of being ostracized, losing their jobs, their businesses, and their stability. Not everybody likes to put their head in the sand, so they can go with the status quo that is popular at that time. This is what was previously discussed when it stated that we live in an upside down, backwards ass society, and no one that is against a "transformation" can voice the facts only to be drowned out with opinions, psychological babble, and false philosophies. They're people who are on the side of being blind, to the principle of facts when it comes to false transformations. You cannot argue with the principle truth especially when it can be proven. The old saying goes, "if it needs an explanation, then it must be your imagination."

It is not insecurity if you do not accept these false transformations, you're just in the tangible reality. Not one person can make you get on the blind fold side of accepting the false realities, that they want everyone else to live. Also, if you are living in the reality, those in their false transformations will make you regret the day that you spoke against them. They will have you living in the operation of F.E.A.R. (False Evidence Appearing Real). This F.E.A.R., is the reason that the people who do not accept these artificial transformations, are fired from their jobs and their businesses suffer. Especially, if you're someone that has celebrity status. They're always on the news because a bunch of protesters are outside the studio that shoots their movies and tv shows. They accept these artificial transformations, because of pressure from their companies to be tolerant of those, that do not accept who they look at in the mirror.

True Identities

That is an anathema to your life. You cannot allow somebody or somebodies to compromise the principle truth that you live daily. Just because you don't agree to an artificial transformation, does not mean you hate it or have an ill rational fear of the "change." It just means that you do not agree to it, nor want to be quite about your disagreements. Guess freedom of speech is no longer the norm in the U.S. Remember when it was discussed in the previous pages about the Sir Isaac Newton ideology, well that ideology can go the same way when someone tries to drown out the disagreement of the "change. For the way that those who wouldn't let you get a word in about why you don't take the position of agreeing to the "change," then don't let them get a word in as well. This is part of the circle of uncompromised principles. Never allow your principles to go the way of the Do-Do bird, just because it takes away that person's comfort. There are a lot of things that go on in this world, that you will never agree with. However, you do not have to put yourself in a position that you'll have to compromise your integrity. Be real with yourself, be honest with yourself and never allow anyone to make you a liar. Especially, when it comes to disagreeing with false changes, false labels and made up progressiveness on a subject that you feel strongly about. Never keep your mouth shut and never bite your tongue. If you cannot agree to disagree in a fashion you can both be civil, then they'll be no reason for you to listen to the drowning sounds of discontent.

In this modern-day society, it seems everyone is living under the delusion that everything natural is a social construct. Such things as: who your identity is, what you are as you were born and how truly you live as you were born. Superman is his identity; Clark Kent is

the disguise. According to the story in the comics, when he came to the Earth from his planet,
he developed his powers. However, to hide this gift, he disguised himself as who he was
around, humans. As his disguise Clark Kent, he was clumsy, powerless and at the mercy of the
limitations of every human that is looking for a "savior." When it was time to save the
powerless humans, he removed his disguise and became his true self: SUPERMAN. This is
something that we must not do so we make everyone else feel comfortable around you. Never
hide your true natural self or the agreement that everything natural is reality, not a made-up
social construct.

Do you know what is feels like to hide your true feelings, about the falsified constructs
that is put in front of our faces? You're afraid to say anything, because you're spearing other
people's feelings of their so-called safe spaces people think they have. Safe spaces from the
truth is a delusion. The truth is, there aren't any safe spaces far enough for anyone to just
agree with you, because it is the societal thing to do. Remember when it was discussed that
we're living in a backward ass society? People think if you paint strips on a lion you can call it a
tiger. I feel like a giraffe. So, should I get my neck elongated, walk on all fours or be exactly
who I'm really supposed to be, as I was born?

Give it to me Straight

I love straight shooters; those are the people who put everybody's feelings to the back
burner. They're the most truthful people that you will ever meet. I have met a lot of those
people in my life and I'm grateful that I've meet those people. If it wasn't for them, I wouldn't

be the bold person I am now. When it comes to certain subjects, no matter how much I disagreed, I was a push over to the point I just agreed with what that person said. The Universe is funny, those people came into my life at the right time, with them I got over that push over BS quick.

They're people who claim to be straight shooters by their words but look for actions. Most of the time those who claim that, are usually the ones who are fake, phony, and not real as they said. Those people would never have the full circle of life because they cannot be real with the person, they're with daily: THEMSELVES. They're the very same people that would tell you that you're wrong, for not agreeing with them on a subject that they feel strongly about. To be the push over, is to be a doormat for those, that are non-intellectual bullies looking for an easy prey. So, they can have a following of yes men and women, that wouldn't call them out when they're wrong. You cannot be the doormat, it gets stepped on, people wipe their feet, dogs use it to roll around on it and it is on the ground. The doormat gets used a lot, to the point where the writing is faded out. Never put yourself in that position, also, never allow anyone outside of you to put you in the position of being faded away. This is part of the circle of never to be used for others so-called facts just to agree with them, with the Cognitive Dissonance that they have.

Everyone in the world are actors. I say this because we're always playing some role that we never auditioned for. Some roles in life are natural roles such as; being a parent, a child, and an adult. Then there are the roles that we must play daily, to make our lives exciting. Roles as, the brave cowards that hide behind the computer screen to cyberbully someone, make fun of a person, use racial epithets to fight with a person of another race and be someone besides themselves. Actors are the world's best liars, they must be someone else daily and make you believe that they are that person, even if those people are fictional. They will play these roles to make everybody believe that they're doing better than the next person, especially if they're online. After they are done with these roles, they must face themselves, and come to the realization that, they are not who they say they were. Also, their lives are not as good as everyone thinks it is. Never play the role of deception, be exactly who you are, you will be respected in the long run, if you're authentic with yourself and with others. Not one person in this world knew if they were being deceived, would have you in their lives. Do not be that person who can't be real with themselves. If you have a person who couldn't be real with themselves, then how would you think that they can be real with you?

You're the Biggest Loser

When you manipulate someone for your own needs and wants, you become the biggest loser. Manipulation is one of the ways to lose those you've build up relationships with. Also, it will have the opposite effect of your goal. I have seen people use all types of manipulative ways to get over on those they perceive as weak. One of the ways that I've seen these manipulative tactics, is when a man and woman go out on a date. The way the manipulation start, is when one of them ask this question: "what are you looking for in a partner"? Then that person tells them their "specifications" of a perfect mate. You without knowing it, opened the door for you to be tricked into being with this person. You just gave them, the ammunition for their manipulative tactics to work. Now you're stuck in a quagmire where there isn't a victory of a relationship, but the defeat of being fooled into your circumstance.

The other way I have seen these manipulation tactics used, was when I used to go to church. People use the verses of their religious text, for people to do their bidding, get with the opposite sex even when they're not interested in you and make you believe in their religion. I remember back in 2012, when I went to church on a Saturday. I was speaking with a friend of mine, she told me about a guy that was talking to her. She really wasn't interested in him, he used the Proverbs pick up line, "he who finds a wife, finds a good thing." I gave the overexaggerated eye roll, as saying, "he really though that would work." This society would be a lot better if we did not resort to manipulation, to achieve ill-gotten goals.

Be on the lookout for Gaslighting, especially when you are in a vulnerable mental state. The people who uses this technique with you, are the ones who have an ulterior motive to control you. It is usually used by abusive spouses, dictators, religious leaders, and those who are in cults. This is used as one of the ultimate manipulation tactics, it makes you deny your own sanity and you will depend on the person who is Gaslighting you.

That is how people follow religious practices, they tell you something is wrong with you. Born into so-called Sin, you're broken, nothing can save you but the belief in this said religion. Be careful with this kind of manipulation, it will have you doing and saying things that you would never have done. The people that rely on this kind of tactic, are the very same ones who would make you feel as if you are wrong, due to the lack of proof of this said belief.

This is how stalkers, rapist and killers can justify what they did to their victims. These

predators will victimize their prey, then have it in their heads, "if that person wasn't dressed a

certain way, if they weren't in that spot, if they just accepted my invitation to go on a date and

if they didn't break up with me, none of this wouldn't of happened". This kind of thinking with

those kinds of people, you do not need to be in the presence of the those who don't have your

best interest at hand. There's an old saying, "a watched pot never boils." This is how you

would know who has your best interest or who will stab you in the back.

On your 6 Points

You can say what you want, but your actions tell another story. If the actions do not

match up with the words they speak, that is called hypocrisy. Those people are not to be

trusted or allowed in your circle. When you think about all the people in your life, how many of

them ever put your needs first for a common goal. If the answer is none, then you'll need a

new circle of company. This is the phase of the circle that you cannot allow hypocrisy,

Gaslighting and manipulation to enter your life.

The philosophy of the Full Circle comes down to the 6 points of life, which need to be

lived by. They are: Life, Love, Loyalty, Knowledge, Wisdom and Understanding. Each point is

60 degrees of the triangular state of the circle, which is around the 2 intersected triangles of

balance. When you draw a line to each point of the intersected triangles, it makes a perfect

circle around the symbol.

In each category is the descriptive view of things to make your seed grow. Like the trees, house plants and gardens need sun, water, dirt, and positive vibrations from our voices to grow. We also need things to grow as well such as, food, water, and the sun. In which, we are like the very fruit and vegetables that we plant. The first of the points of the Full Circle is Life.

This is the beginning of all things manifested in the tangible existence. The first touch and taste of the energy called food. Your first smile, first steps and the beginning of many things in your existence that will be wonderous. This is the starting point of the growth that we, must go through as the seedlings of the fertile soil garden of plentiful crops that is us. The point of Life is to go through stages of Growth and Development of your dreams, to manifest in the tangible reality. There will be things that we will go through, situations will happen with us, that will be in this life. We must grow with the time we are in and let the events play out in its entirety.

As Life, will only stress you out to the point of no return. When you allow people, things and the emotions of misery and disgust affect you. Never allow these things to tear down the House that you built, to crumble under the destruction of these issues. The stresses of whatever comes, you should treat like water in a strainer. As long the bowl doesn't fill, the water will always drain out in a sea of forgettable destinations.

The second point of the circle is Love. This emotional action is needed, to express our feelings in an intimate way. It is without conditions or fear of reprisals, if you don't fulfill the natural contract for the unlimited acceptance that is asked of you. The connection of this Love is universal with every race, creed, ethnicity, religious beliefs, and acts of physical and

emotional stabilities that we hold to our societal normalcy. Natural Love can come in many

forms such as verbal, physical, emotional, and mental. As the lioness hunts for her children to

eat, the lion protects the pride. We will do anything for our families, friends, and partners.

It can be a simple word, comfort, waking them up to pull them out of the void of despair

or a touch to let them know that you're always there. This is the point in which the seeds from

Life, come into fruition and manifest into something great. The sincerity from the bottom of

one's heart, is when no matter what happens you will always have love for that person.

However, there will be a time, even when the love for that person, will make it hard to walk

away.

The next is Loyalty. This is the third point of the existence that is needed for our

families, friends and loved ones. To water your plants of stability and to feed it with the food of

the soil it's planted in. To be loyal to yourself, is to show Loyalty to others. In a way that no

matter what, you will always be by their side through the thickest and thinnest of times.

Loyalty is the cornerstone, which shows you won't hold onto any grudges for past issues in

relationships. To mend the wounds of the bullet holes that were left behind, after the shots

were fired.

Also, Loyalty is to be faithful, even when the other person has contracted the disease

called, "the hypocrisy of letting go." Loyalty is a part of the 3 points of completion of balance, is

what we all need, for the half of the completed 6 points. It can be a wonderful experience, only if it's placed in the right hands. However, if you're loyal to the wrong thing or person, it would be a pointless pursuit to hold on to it. Just like if you would put a band-aid on a .357 bullet wound, you'll just be covering up the wound, but it will never heal.

The fourth point of the circle is Knowledge. This feeds the soul of intellectual yearning, to know all things that you can use to maneuver in the maze of life. You gain this Knowledge by many branches of the trees, which is grown in the forest of mandatory learning. About how things work in the beginning, how to speak the language of your ancestors and to read the books that were written by those, who left behind the essence of their souls. Knowledge is like lifting weights, you'll gain more strength the longer you do it. You'll be able to take on more of the pounds of fundamental learning. To have Knowledge of yourself, it something that can never be taken away. Also, it's the fire of the essence that can burn any building of self-doubt and build you up to self-sufficiency. There people in this society that think they have Knowledge, but they are just knowing. There's not much I can say about the Knowledge part of the 6 points, that you as the reader haven't discovered for yourself.

The fifth point of the circle is Wisdom. The Wisdom that is each and one of us is to have the forethought of a situation, then to look at it logically. Also, to analyze the root of the issue before it becomes the weeds of the fertile soil of your garden. Many centuries ago, Wisdom was sought after more than riches. Kings and Queens consulted with wisemen, for the way they can look at an object or an event, to give them the answers. Also, they spread their wisdom with proverbs and analogies, so the layman had the idea to interpret what they were saying. That is why, when someone try to explain something that can go over other people's heads, they break it down in Layman's Terms.

Wisdom is another part of the circle, which is the building block of the DNA life cycle. Without it, you will have a defect of the stability that is life within you. This is the meaning of soaking up information to make decisions in life. The Wisdom that is set in front of you, to use as a tool to foresee circumstances of decisions, that we must make and have the choices of those decisions of life. There is an old saying, "The Wise knows how not to speak and appear intelligent, but the fool speaks and removes all doubt of stupidity."

When you use Wisdom in its purest form, you will realize that the things you may have knew in the tangible existence, is a false dichotomy of knowledge. With Wisdom, you will realize that daily you need to be in the correct state of mind. Also, you will know the difference between a tomato growing on a vine, the Wisdom to know that tomato is a fruit and the Understanding that tomatoes do not belong in a fruit salad. Which brings the last part of the completion of the last point of the inverted triangles is Understanding.

This is the completion of the 360 degrees. We started with Love, then Life, Loyalty, Knowledge, Wisdom and finally Understanding. This comes with the 5-time rule, which is when you hear something 5 times, it finally sticks to your thought process. Also, having the Understanding, to realize that not everything is what it seems to be on the surface. When you look at the pictures on social media sites, do you think that is the real life they're living. On my

Facebook pages on the news feed, I put one of my quotes on there. I said, "People look happy

in pictures, but no one ever sees the black eye under the makeup."

That saying does put things in perspective when it comes to the point of

Understanding. When you look at the pictures of those in still moments, pictures of the happy

times, relationships, and old friends, that time as passed. The frozen moments are there as

reminders of what we had and the years we lived.   Also, you think a person is living their best

life in those pictures. However, what you do not see, is the hand that is being twisted behind

someone's back. When Understanding is put with the true context of comprehending the

lessons that you were taught, then you will have the tools to see all aspects of everything you

come across, when things seem not to match with would you discovered about yourself. Then

you may come across someone else's need, to block you with their Confirmation Bias opinion of

you.

Writing this book, they're a lot of things I now Understand. There were events that

happened in my life, that there are things that I can no longer do. In pursuit of self-happiness, I

now Understand that I can no longer give privileges to those who think it is a right to have

them. When you come to that Understanding, your life will change, you will never be the same.

We as a people must take into consideration that in life, things must play out in its

entirety. It does take a process of Cause and Effect. They are no immediate results, when you

plant a seed, it will not bear fruit on the same day. A child will not develop into an adult in a

day. Even in the Bible, the god of it did not supposedly create the universe in one day. When you think in that aspect, of the continuous stream of the process in which we call life, you will Understand that everything takes a process.

Even the seasons that comes yearly, has a gradual transition. With this transition you will have different types of understandings, that you must have to get ready for the next evolution of the life you're about to go through. With these transitions, also comes the regret of things that happened in the time you lived. When you look back of the choices that you made and the actions that you done, do you ever ask yourself, "did I make the right decisions"?

If you must ask yourself that question, then you have regrets in the transitions in your life. We make the decisions, that we think is the best for us at that time. It could be a job that you wanted, but then found out that the business is not what you thought. A relationship that you were in, however come to find that the relationship you had was not the best one for you. Moving into a house on an apartment you thought because it was in a good neighborhood the grass was greener, but then you smelled the manure. Therefore, we must look at every situation to think, if I would kill this one thing, will it save me from a thousand issues.

We all Have Them

When we have regrets about what we done, that is one of those, "if hindsight was 20/20" categories. We did not know that our decisions in the transition of life, would affect our future. In this Understanding, we must make our moves to be 2 steps in front of us, so we must not have these regrets to look back on. They are things that brings regrets to the front, also we need to question ourselves, "is this something that I would look back on and feel bad about it."

I have seen movies that when people commit a crime against another person, then try to justify to themselves of why they did what they did. I was watching a movie called, "I Spit on Your Grave." The remake not the original. Five guys violated this woman and tried to kill her, but she got them all back. They were full of I'm sorry and I didn't mean to do it, they had regrets when the rabbit got the gun. The transition that she went through, first she was a writer that came to the cabin in the woods, then she was the hand of her own vengeance. Not one person on this Earth was born with anger, hate, disgust, regrets and with a mind state to hurt their fellow human being.

This is when you say, "something had to happened to that person." When a person is depressed, hurt, angry, and overall unhappy, it had to be cause by something that is outside of themselves. Where the transition comes in, is when you heal from the causes of others, the regret comes in you think, "I should have done this sooner." When we allow regrets to take over our thought process, then we become the ones who is shattered with the broken glass of misery. Life is full of risks and regrets, it is of the broken circle of the tranquility of the mind, body, and soul. So much so, it becomes the abyss of emptiness that is the wasted of looking back at past failures.

Whether it is a marriage that didn't work out, a job you lost or the life that was wasted by thinking about the regrets of days past. Me personally, everything I did, is not anything that I have regrets about. I look back at the things that happened in my life and there were situations that I did put myself in. I do not look at them with regrets in my heart, I look at these things as, "it happened, oh well, move on to the next."

I went through transitions while I was writing this book. During the writing of this book, I have broken up with the girl that I was with. Let's just say that relationship was not what everybody thought. I do not regret a minute of what I did. As it was discussed in the earlier chapters, everything that a person does, it was them that ultimately made that decision and performed that action. For a minute I was happy, I thought we were on the same level when it came to life goals. I went to Canada to visit her. Also, that was my first time going to the place I went to, not the country itself. I spent 4 days up there and it was ok, but it could have been better, if I had better company. There were some red flags that were in earlier relationships, that I didn't pay attention to. This time, I did pay attention to them and broke up with her. I did not regret that decision.

The regrets that we have, is not something that we should hold on to. The person that has regrets of things that is already done and over with, is the same person who would tell you that someone else's fault that those things happen. However, they're the ones who did those things. This is for the broken that has the Understanding transition, who can pick up the broken pieces. When the broken vase of regrets shatters on the floor of life, pick up the pieces and fix them. Then you can look back and say, "regrets are for the weak."

Going back to the Understanding of how life transitions from one point to another. The process that was spoken of, is something that we must go through. To realize it is never anything quick, that these transitions to the end happen. Coming to the end of this journey of this book, it all comes together with the beginning and the end. Also, whether it be the termination of a relationship, job or moving into another apartment or house. These things are inevitable, nothing is forever. Not even the lives we live. YOLO (you only live once), the saying should be YLD and YODO, (you live daily) (you only die once). It is a literal fact of life; we live many days, but we die once. There's always a restart of the life cycles that we go through. We see the restart every day, when children are born, when we find a new house, a new job, and a new relationship.

In the first pages of this book, it was said that life is a circle. It means even though life is a circle, it will continuously live on. With the memories of those who are still here that knew you. Your descendants and everything you touched, will have the fingerprints of your essence. Even those who do not have direct descendants, others will know that you were here. I end this chapter by saying this; everywhere you go, everything that you do, leave your mark. When people remember you let it be a good memory. So, when people think about you, it will leave a smile on their faces, with tears of joy. They will say, "it wasn't a long time that this person was here, but when they were it was a good time."

THE END OF THIS JOURNEY. STARTING THE NEXT.

EPILOGUE

How was this journey? Did this book take you through loops? Did it offend you in any way? The things in this book, were shared through stories, sayings and just a little education. As if you didn't already know these things. There are many journeys that we partake on. However, no matter how many different beginnings that we have, they all have a universal truth. They all begin with one step.

Even though this is a short book, in my eyes, I hope the reader will get something from it. I hope you have insight, into the mind of the author. The philosophy that was spoken about is something we've all have heard. Through years of trying to find ourselves, little did we know we didn't have to look further than the mirror.

Be on the lookout for other books, for my FULL CIRCLE catalog. Next Book: The Human Deception. This one will be a little controversial with the reader. However, what will be said in this book, does have to be said. This book is going to be risk but then again, life is a risk every day we wake up.

ACKNOWLEDGEMENTS

First, I like to thank the Universal Source for bringing my creators and for them creating me. I dedicate this book to my mother Luevenia Ann Byas. 1959 to 2019. Also, to my brothers Russell Bolar, Tony Mitchell, Eddie Jarell Byas. Till the world blow, till the casket drop, we will always have love for one another. That goes for my sister as well Natasha Shantae. One Love. I also like to give thanks to Adele J. Foster-Glenn, for teaching me about the fine art of self-publishing. Also, for helping me reunite with my passion of writing. With that I also like to thank Christianna Wright and yes, I'm using your full Gov'ment. We been through thick and thin with each other. To all those I consider family to Illinois to Texas and the states between. Also like to thank C1 for teaching me how to innovate. To all the members of the BYAS family never separated and forever growing. To my nieces and nephews, also great-nieces and nephews, damn I'm old. Last, I like to thank the Earth for the daily inspiration of people, places, and things.

References:

The Holy Bible, New King James Version. Nashville: Nelson. 1982. ISBN 978-0840700537.

"New King James Version (NKJV Bible)". The Bible Gateway. Retrieved 2011-09-14.

"The Curious Case of Benjamin Button" (1921) (in Tales of the Jazz Age) ISBN 978-0-521-402Merriam-Webster Dictionary". Encyclopedia Britannica Online. 2015. Retrieved June 24, 2015.38-5

"Too $hort:: Life is... Too $hort :: Jive/Zomba". Rapreviews.com. 2003-05-02. Retrieved 2015-07-25.